A SCOTT FORESMAN Adventure

Reading STREET

Reading STREET

Indiana

Program Authors

Peter Afflerbach	Jeanne Paratore
Camille Blachowicz	P. David Pearson
Candy Dawson Boyd	Sam Sebesta
Wendy Cheyney	Deborah Simmons
Connie Juel	Sharon Vaughn
Edward Kame'enui	Susan Watts-Taffe
Donald Leu	Karen Kring Wixson

PEARSON
Scott Foresman

Editorial Offices: Glenview, Illinois • Parsippany, New Jersey • New York, New York
Sales Offices: Boston, Massachusetts • Duluth, Georgia • Glenview, Illinois
Coppell, Texas • Sacramento, California • Mesa, Arizona

We dedicate Reading Street to
Peter Jovanovich.

His wisdom, courage,
and passion for education
are an inspiration to us all.

About the Cover Artist

When Scott Gustafson was in grade school, he spent most of his spare time drawing pictures. Now he gets to make pictures for a living. Before he starts a painting, he photographs his family, pets, or friends posing as characters that will appear in the illustration. He then uses the photos to inspire the finished picture. In this cover you can see his pet cockatiel, Piper.

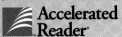

Dear Indiana Reader,

A new school year is beginning. Are you ready? You are about to take a trip along a famous street—*Scott Foresman Reading Street.* During this trip you will travel in space with some astronauts. You will explore the desert. You will go camping with Henry and his big dog Mudge. You will even build a robot with good friends Pearl and Wagner.

As you read these stories and articles, you will learn new things that will help you in science and social studies.

While you are enjoying these exciting pieces of literature, you will find that something else is going on—you are becoming a better reader.

Have a great trip, and don't forget to write!

Sincerely,
The Authors

Exploration

What can we learn from exploring new places and things?

Read It ONLINE
sfsuccessnet.com

Working Together

How can we work together?

Read It
ONLINE
sfsuccessnet.com

Creative Ideas

What does it mean to be creative?

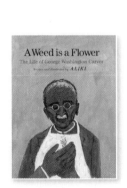

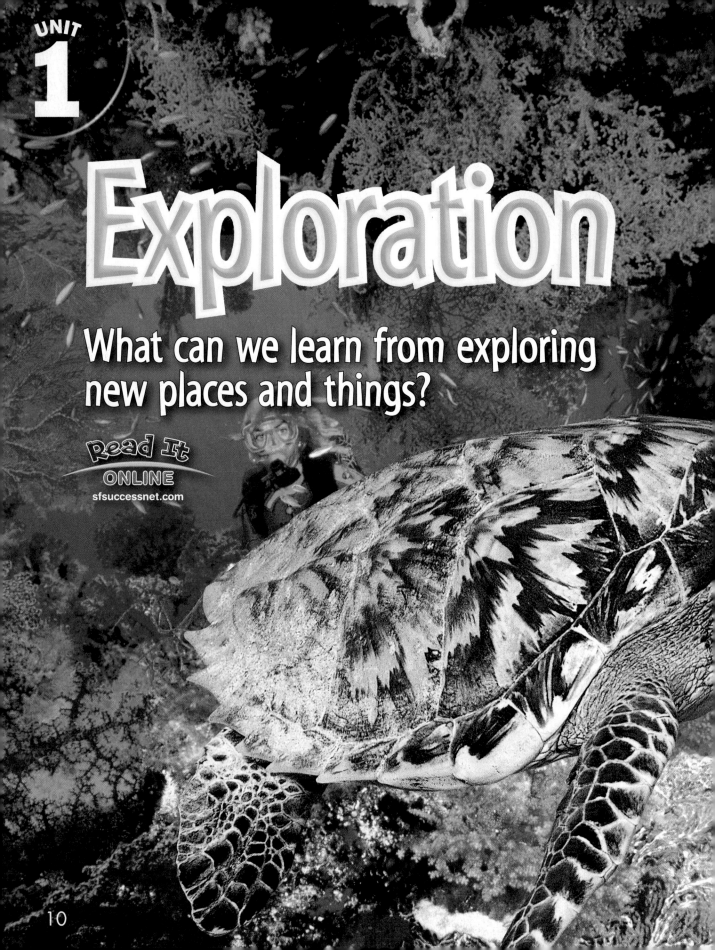

Exploration

What can we learn from exploring new places and things?

Read It
ONLINE
sfsuccessnet.com

Let's Talk About
EXPLORATION

Words to Read

country
beautiful
front
someone
somewhere
friend

14

Read the Words

Iris and her family have moved to the country. It is a beautiful place. Iris looked at the long road in front of her house. She hopes that someone out there somewhere is waiting to be her friend.

Genre: Realistic Fiction
Realistic fiction is a made-up story that could happen in real life. Now read about Iris, a girl who moves to the country and finds a new friend.

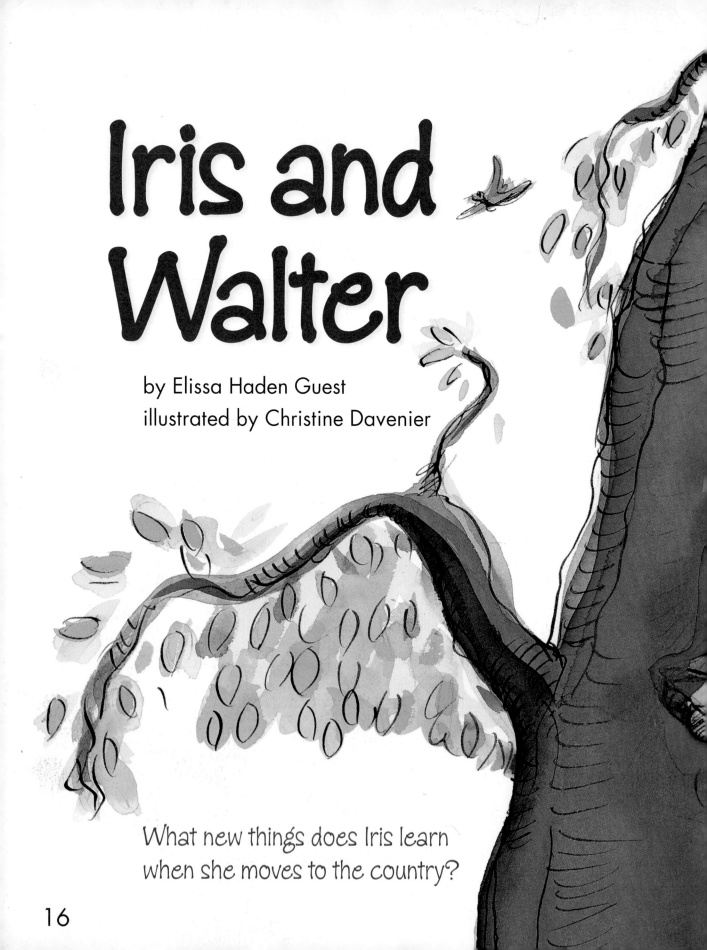

Iris and Walter

by Elissa Haden Guest

illustrated by Christine Davenier

What new things does Iris learn
when she moves to the country?

18

A Walk and a Talk

Iris and Grandpa went for a walk.

"Can I tell you something?" Iris asked.

"You can tell me anything," said Grandpa.

"I hate the country," said Iris.

"Why?" asked Grandpa.

"Because there are no children here,"
said Iris. "The country is as lonely as Mars."

"Iris, my girl, there must be some
children somewhere," said Grandpa.
"Do you think so?" asked Iris.
"I know so. We shall have
to find them, Iris. We shall
be explorers!"

Iris and Grandpa walked
down the road. The birds
were singing. The roses were
blooming. And around the
bend, someone was waiting.

21

Iris and Grandpa walked around the
bend. They saw a great big green tree.
"What a tree!" said Grandpa.
"So green!" said Iris.
"So beautiful," said Grandpa.
"I want to climb it," said Iris.

Down came a ladder.

23

"Amazing! I wonder what's up there?" said Grandpa.

"I'll go see," said Iris. Iris began to climb.

"How is it up there?" called Grandpa.

"It's very green!" yelled Iris.

Iris climbed higher and higher until she was almost at the top of the great big green tree.

"Grandpa?!" called Iris.
"There's a house up here."
"Amazing!" said Grandpa.

25

Iris knocked on the door.

"Come in," said a voice.

Iris opened the door.

"Hi, I'm Walter," said Walter.

"I'm Iris," said Iris.

Iris and Walter shook hands.

"Hey, Grandpa, there's a kid up here named Walter!" yelled Iris.

"How wonderful," said Grandpa.

And it was.

A New Life

Iris and Walter played every day. They climbed trees. They rolled down hills. They played hide-and-seek.

When it rained, Walter showed Iris his hat collection. And Iris showed Walter how to roller-skate—indoors.

Some days they rode Walter's sweet pony, Sal. Other days they sat on a fence and watched a horse named Rain running wild.

"Tell me about the big city," said Walter.

"Well," said Iris, "in the big city, there are lots and lots and lots of people."

"Ah," said Walter. "But in the country there are lots and lots and lots of stars."

Iris and Walter played every day. But still Iris dreamed of the big city. She dreamed of her noisy street and her wide front stoop.

She dreamed of tango music and of
roller-skating down long hallways.
But Iris was not sad.

3

For in the country, there were
red-tailed hawks and starry skies.

There were pale roses. And there was
cool grass beneath her feet. There was a
wild horse named Rain and a sweet pony
named Sal.

And across the meadow,
over the stream, high in a tree,
was a little house. And inside
there was a new friend. . . Walter.

Think and Share

Talk About It Stories can go on and on. What do you think Iris and Walter do next?

1. Use the pictures below to retell the story.

2. Where does *Iris and Walter* take place? How might the story be different if Iris and Walter had met in the city?

3. What did you predict Iris would find in the tree? Were you right? What other predictions did you make?

Look Back and Write Look back at page 19. What problem did Iris have? How did that change? Use details from the story to help you.

Meet the Author and Illustrator
Elissa Haden Guest

STARRING
ELISSA HADEN GUEST

Elissa Haden Guest likes big cities. She says, "New York was a very exciting place to grow up. You can walk for miles there without getting tired or bored because there's so much to see. Many of the streets are crowded with people and there's this terrific energy in the air."

Read more books about Iris and Walter.

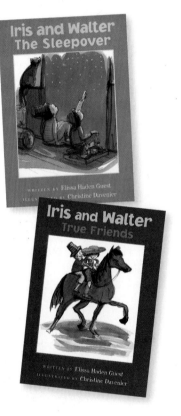

Christine Davenier

Christine Davenier lives in France, where she grew up. She taught kindergarten for four years before attending art school. She has illustrated many children's books.

Morning Song

by Bobbi Katz

Today is a day to catch tadpoles.
Today is a day to explore.
Today is a day to get started.
Come on! Let's not sleep anymore.

Outside the sunbeams are dancing.
The leaves sing a rustling song.
Today is a day for adventures,
and I hope that you'll come along!

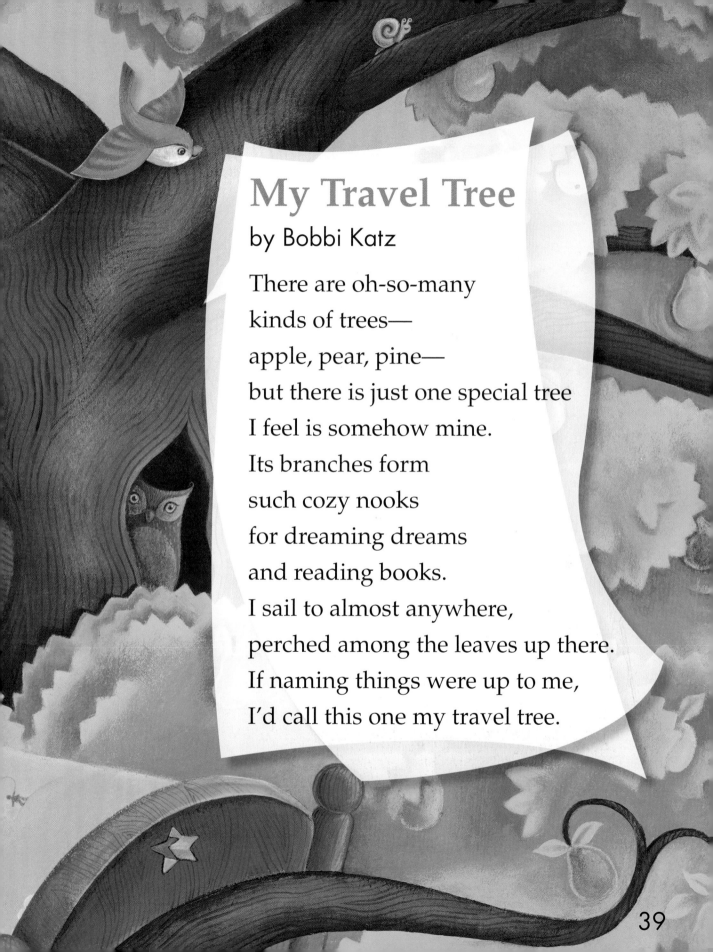

My Travel Tree
by Bobbi Katz

There are oh-so-many
kinds of trees—
apple, pear, pine—
but there is just one special tree
I feel is somehow mine.
Its branches form
such cozy nooks
for dreaming dreams
and reading books.
I sail to almost anywhere,
perched among the leaves up there.
If naming things were up to me,
I'd call this one my travel tree.

Sentences

A **sentence** is a group of words that tells a complete idea. The words are in an order that makes sense. A sentence begins with a capital letter. Many sentences end with a **period (.)**.

Iris and Walter went swimming.

This is a sentence. It tells a complete idea.

Sal the pony.

This is not a sentence. It does not tell a complete idea. It needs to tell what Sal the pony does or is.

Write Using Sentences

1. This is not a sentence.

Iris and Walter.

Make it a sentence. Tell something that Iris and Walter do. Don't forget to use a period.

- -

2. Choose a sentence from the story that tells about the pony or the horse. Tell more about the animal you choose. Be sure your sentence tells a complete idea.

- -

3. Write some sentences about a special time you had with your family or friends. Remember to begin and end each sentence correctly.

Let's Talk About

EXPLORATION

Words to Read

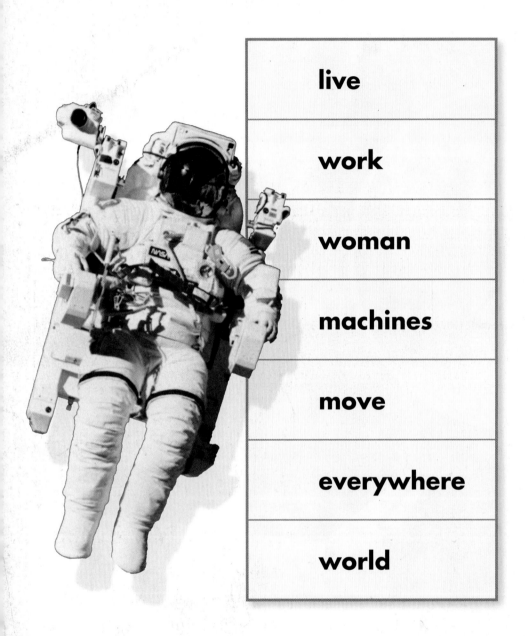

live
work
woman
machines
move
everywhere
world

Read the Words

Astronauts live and work in space.
A woman can be an astronaut.

Machines in space
can move
large things.

Stars are everywhere.
Can you see our world?

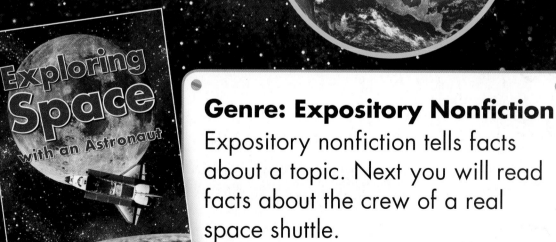

Exploring
Space
with an Astronaut

Genre: Expository Nonfiction
Expository nonfiction tells facts
about a topic. Next you will read
facts about the crew of a real
space shuttle.

Exploring Space

with an Astronaut

by Patricia J. Murphy

What will you find out about space from an astronaut?

Lift-off!

3 . . . 2 . . . 1 . . . Lift-off!

A space shuttle climbs high into the sky. Inside the shuttle, astronauts are on their way to learn more about space.

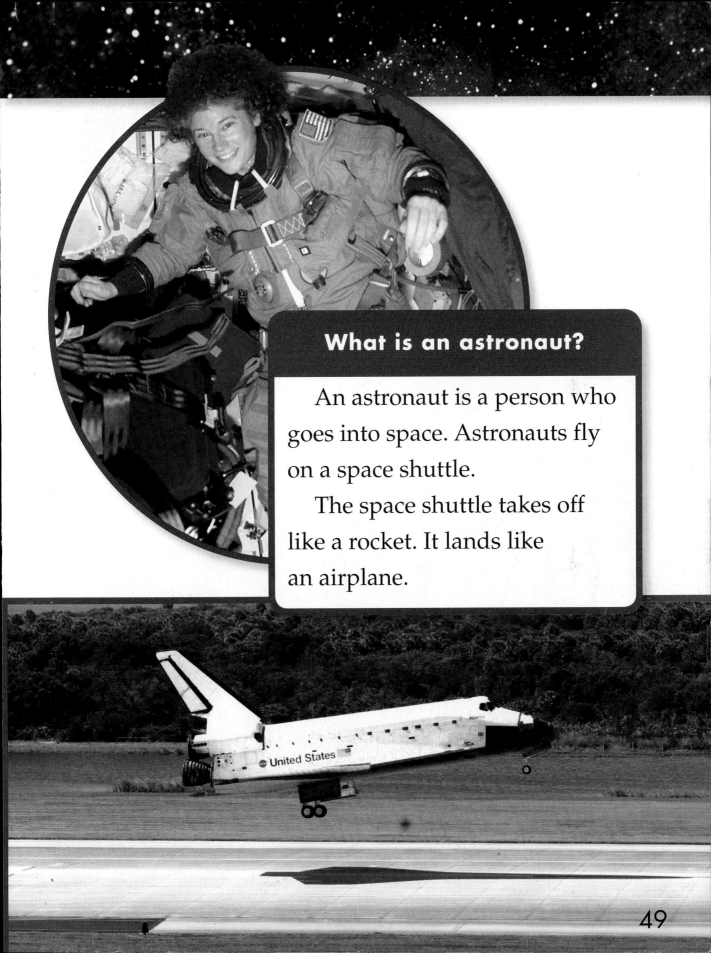

What is an astronaut?

An astronaut is a person who goes into space. Astronauts fly on a space shuttle.

The space shuttle takes off like a rocket. It lands like an airplane.

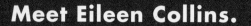
Meet Eileen Collins.

Eileen Collins is an astronaut. She was the first woman to be a space shuttle pilot. She was also the first woman to be the leader of a space shuttle trip.

She and four other astronauts worked as a team. Some astronauts flew the space shuttle. Others did experiments.

How do astronauts live in space?

In the space shuttle, astronauts float everywhere. Sleeping bags are tied to walls. Toilets have a type of seat belt.

Astronauts exercise to stay strong. They take sponge baths to keep clean.

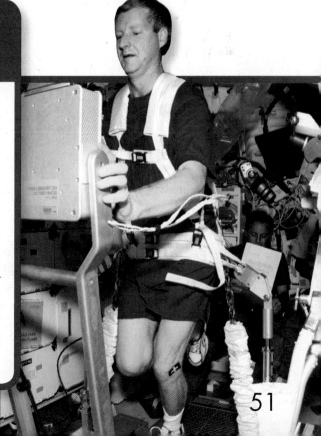

51

Astronauts test ways to live and work in a world that is very different from Earth. In space, there is no up and down, no air, and the sun always shines.

Astronauts do experiments. They look for problems and fix them. This will make space travel safer.

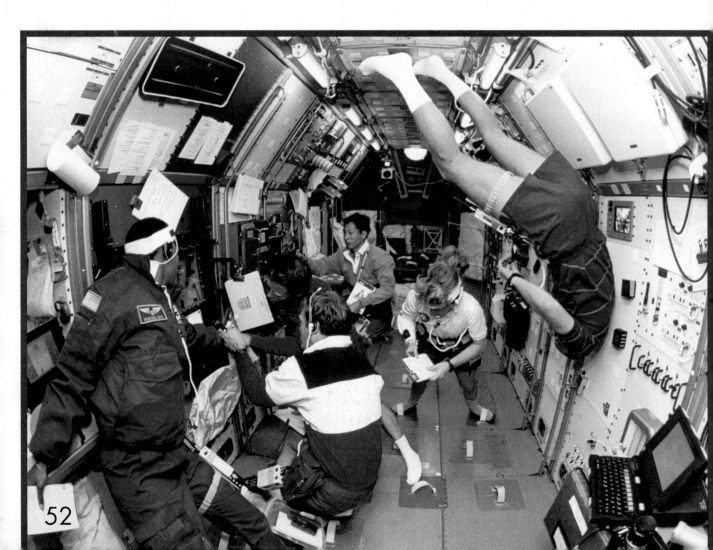

53

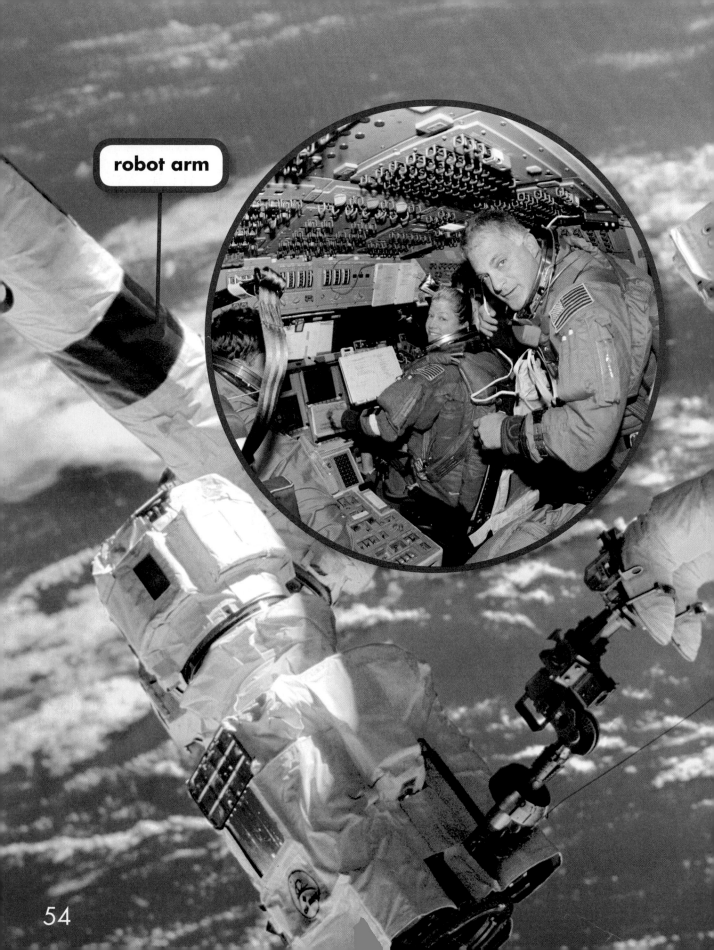

robot arm

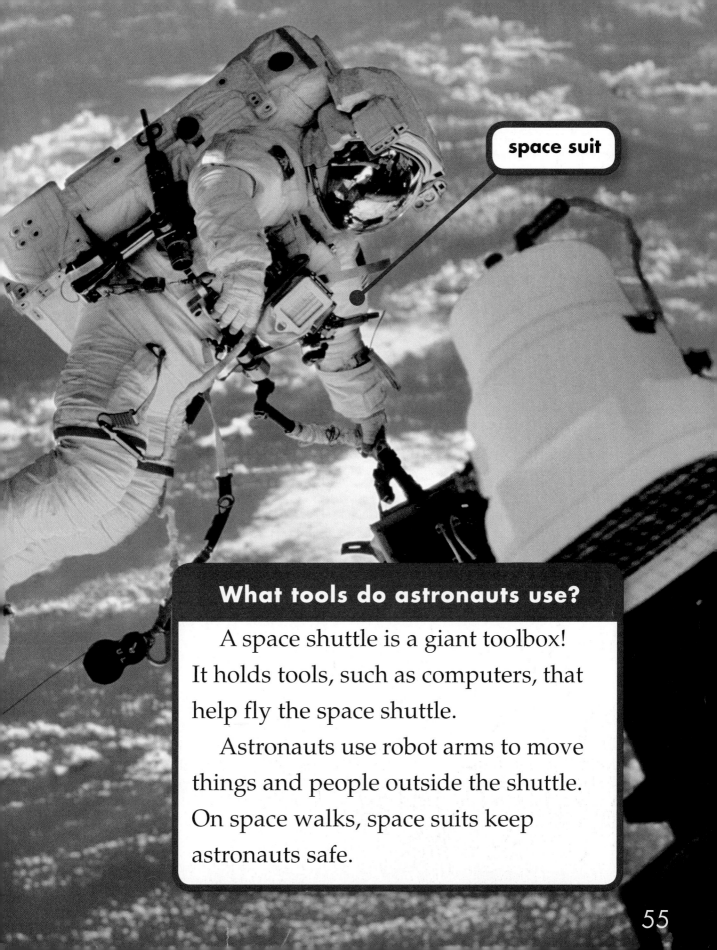

space suit

What tools do astronauts use?

A space shuttle is a giant toolbox! It holds tools, such as computers, that help fly the space shuttle.

Astronauts use robot arms to move things and people outside the shuttle. On space walks, space suits keep astronauts safe.

X-ray telescope named *Chandra*

X-ray telescope

space shuttle

The crew's special job

Eileen Collins and her crew had a special job to do. They took an X-ray telescope into space with them.

First, they tested the telescope. Next, they flipped some switches and let the telescope go into space. Then, the telescope used its rockets to fly higher into space.

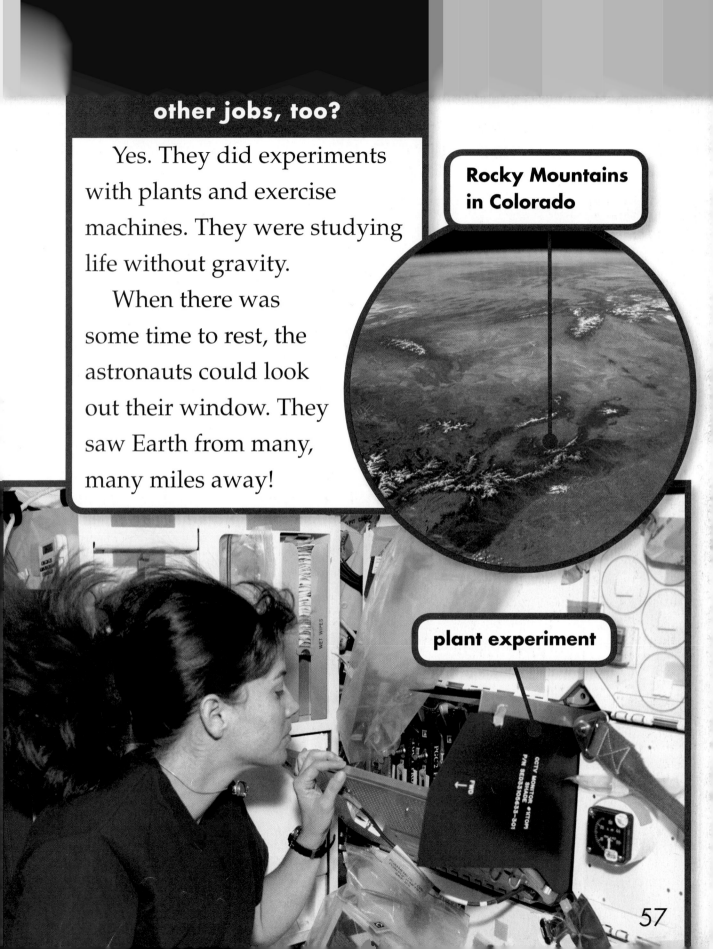

other jobs, too?

Yes. They did experiments with plants and exercise machines. They were studying life without gravity.

When there was some time to rest, the astronauts could look out their window. They saw Earth from many, many miles away!

Rocky Mountains in Colorado

plant experiment

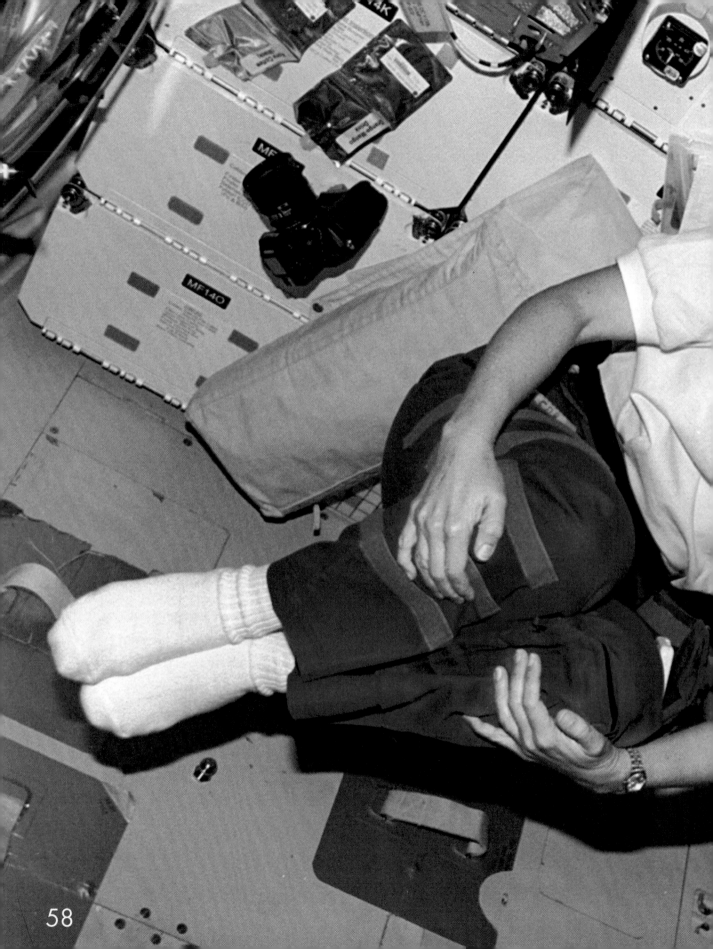

Would you like to fly into space?

Do you like math and science? Do you like to visit new places? Do you like fast roller coasters? Astronauts do, too! Maybe someday you will become an astronaut, just like Eileen Collins.

Think and Share

Talk About It You are an astronaut. Send a one-minute message to Earth. Tell about your trip.

1. Use the pictures below to summarize what you read about astronauts.

2. What do you think is the most important thing the author wanted you to know?

3. Most sections of this selection begin with a question. The next part answers the question. How did that format help you as you read?

Look Back and Write If you really want to be an astronaut, what things should you like? Look back on page 59 to help you answer.

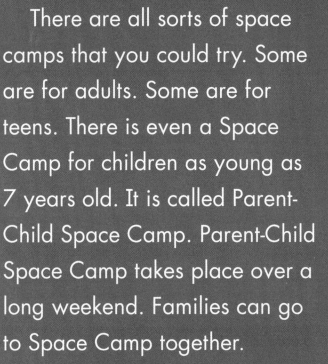

There are all sorts of space camps that you could try. Some are for adults. Some are for teens. There is even a Space Camp for children as young as 7 years old. It is called Parent-Child Space Camp. Parent-Child Space Camp takes place over a long weekend. Families can go to Space Camp together.

Space Camp uses some of the same machines used to train real astronauts. There's a special chair that makes you feel like you are walking on the moon. Another chair is like the kind that astronauts use when they go outside their rocket ship to fix something. A third kind of chair makes you feel like you're floating in space. Still another machine spins you in circles and flips you head over heels. Then there's the Space Shot. The Space Shot shoots you straight into the air at about 45 to 50 miles per hour. You fall back down just as fast. Then you bump up and down a few times before it's over.

Y6 Gravity Chair

Working in Space

A Multi-Axis Giro

Everyone at space camp works together on special missions. On these missions you'll do work like real astronauts do in space. You might get to fly a rocket ship. It's only pretend, of course. You won't really fly into space. But it looks and feels like the real thing. And that's really fun!

Moon Gravity Chair

Subjects

The **subject** of a sentence tells who or what does something.

An astronaut goes into space.

An astronaut is the subject of the sentence.

Eileen Collins piloted the shuttle.

Eileen Collins is the subject of the sentence.

Write Using Subjects

1. Write a sentence from the selection. Underline the subject.

• •

2. Choose a picture from the selection. Write a sentence about the picture. Underline the subject.

• •

3. Astronauts do many everyday things aboard the space shuttle. Write some sentences about what you do every day. Underline the subject of each sentence you write.

Let's Talk About
Exploration

Words to Read

love
mother
father
straight
bear
couldn't
build

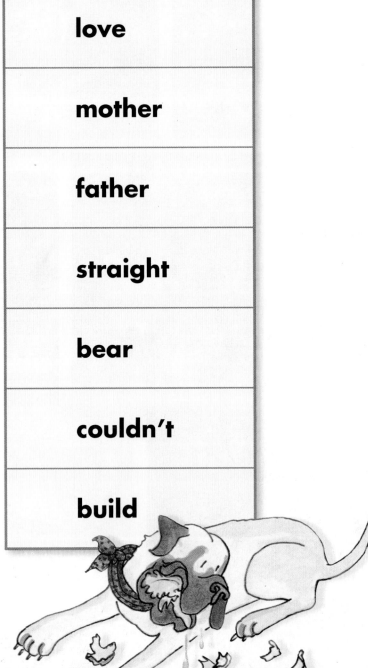

Read the Words

We all love camping. My mother and father take us camping every year. We go straight to the woods when we get there. Something new always happens on these trips. Last year, we saw a bear! I couldn't believe it. This year, my dad promised to teach us how to build a campfire. I can't wait!

Genre: Realistic Fiction Realistic fiction means that a story could happen. Next read about Henry and his dog, Mudge, and, their camping trip.

Henry
and Mudge
and the Starry Night

by Cynthia Rylant
illustrated by Suçie Stevenson

What will Henry and Mudge
find on a starry night?

Contents

Big Bear Lake

In August Henry and Henry's big
dog Mudge always went camping.
They went with Henry's parents.

Henry's mother had been a Camp Fire Girl, so she knew all about camping.

She knew how to set up a tent.

She knew how to build a campfire. She knew how to cook camp food.

Henry's dad didn't know anything about camping. He just came with a guitar and a smile.

Henry and Mudge loved camping. This year they were going to Big Bear Lake, and Henry couldn't wait.

"We'll see deer, Mudge," Henry said.
Mudge wagged.

"We'll see raccoons," said Henry.
Mudge shook Henry's hand.

"We might even see a *bear*," Henry said. Henry was not so sure he wanted to see a bear. He shivered and put an arm around Mudge.

Mudge gave a big, slow, *loud* yawn. He drooled on Henry's foot.

Henry giggled. "No bear will get *us*, Mudge," Henry said. "We're too *slippery!*"

A Good Smelly Hike

Henry and Mudge and Henry's parents drove
to Big Bear Lake. They parked the car and got
ready to hike.

Everyone had a backpack, even Mudge.
(His had lots of crackers.) Henry's mother said,
"Let's go!" And off they went.

They walked and walked and climbed and climbed. It was beautiful.

Henry saw a fish jump straight out of a stream. He saw a doe and her fawn. He saw waterfalls and a rainbow.

Mudge didn't see much of anything. He was smelling. Mudge loved to hike and smell. He smelled a raccoon from yesterday. He smelled a deer from last night.

He smelled an oatmeal cookie from Henry's back pocket. "Mudge!" Henry laughed, giving Mudge the cookie.

Finally Henry's mother picked a good place to camp.

Henry's parents set up the tent. Henry
unpacked the food and pans and lanterns. Mudge
unpacked a ham sandwich. Finally the camp was
almost ready. It needed just one more thing:
"Who knows the words to 'Love Me Tender'?"
said Henry's father with a smile, pulling out his
guitar. Henry looked at Mudge and groaned.

Green Dreams

It was a beautiful night.

Henry and Henry's parents lay on their backs
by the fire and looked at the sky. Henry didn't
know there were so many stars in the sky.

"There's the Big Dipper," said Henry's mother.

"There's the Little Dipper," said Henry.

"There's E. T.," said Henry's dad.

Mudge wasn't looking at stars. He was chewing
on a log. He couldn't get logs this good at home.
Mudge loved camping.

Henry's father sang one more sappy love song, then everyone went inside the tent to sleep. Henry's father and mother snuggled. Henry and Mudge snuggled.

It was as quiet as quiet could be. Everyone slept safe and sound, and there were no bears, no scares. Just the clean smell of trees . . . and wonderful green dreams.

Think and Share

Talk About It Pretend you are Mudge. What were the best sights and smells on the camping trip?

1. Look at the pictures below. They are in the wrong order. Reorder them to retell the story.

2. Who are the characters in this story? Describe the setting.

3. Did anything in this story confuse you? What did you do about it?

Look Back and Write Look at page 76. Who knew all about camping? What did that person do to help with the camping trip? Use details from the story.

Meet the Author and the Illustrator
Cynthia Rylant

Cynthia Rylant never read many books when she was young. There was no library in her town.

Read more books by Cynthia Rylant.

After college, Ms. Rylant worked in a library. "Within a few weeks, I fell in love with children's books," she says. She has written over 60 books!

Suçie Stevenson

Suçie Stevenson has drawn pictures for most of the Henry and Mudge books. Her brother's Great Dane, Jake, was her inspiration for Mudge.

Star Pictures in the Sky

by Lorraine McCombs

Have you ever connected the dots to make a picture? Think about the stars in the sky. A long time ago, people saw the stars as dots in the night sky. They imagined lines going from star to star. They called these star pictures *constellations.*

On a very dark night away from the city, we can see hundreds of stars in the sky. We can even see the same constellations that people saw long ago. Here are a few of them.

This star picture, or constellation, is called Orion. It is named after a famous hunter in Greek stories. We see Orion best in the winter sky. This constellation has three stars in a row. They are thought of as Orion's belt.

The Big Dipper is a star picture in the constellation called Big Bear. We can see the Big Dipper any time of the year, but it is best seen between January and October. Two stars in the Big Dipper point toward the very bright North Star.

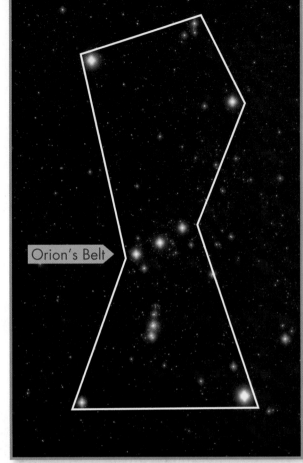

Orion's Belt

Orion

Big Dipper

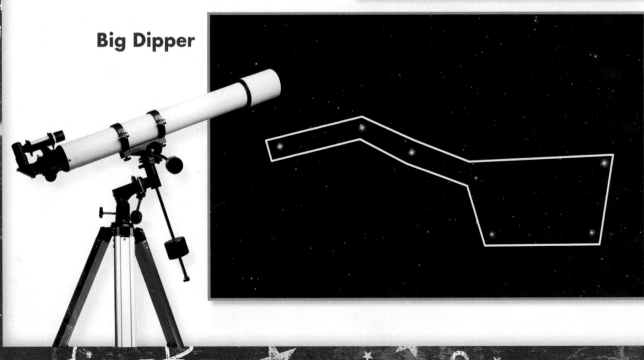

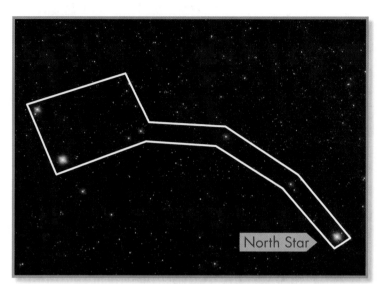

Little Dipper

Big Dog

Another star picture is the Little Dipper. You can see the Little Dipper all year. Notice the handle. The brightest star in the handle is the North Star. It never moves. For hundreds of years, people have used the North Star to find their way.

Canis was a dog in Greek stories. *Canis* means "dog," and this constellation is known as the Big Dog. The very bright star is called the Dog Star. It is the brightest star in our whole nighttime sky. You can usually find this constellation in the summer sky between July and September.

The next time you look up at a dark, starry sky, think about these constellations. Connect the dots as people did long ago. What star pictures do you see?

Predicates

The **predicate** tells what the subject of a sentence does or is.

Henry and Mudge **walked down the trail.**

The words **walked down the trail** tell what Henry and Mudge did.

Henry's mom **is a hiker.**

The words **is a hiker** tell what Henry's mom is.

Write Using Predicates

1. Write a sentence from the story. Underline the predicate.

. . . .

2. What would you do on a camping trip? Write a sentence about it. Underline the predicate in your sentence.

. . . .

3. Write about a trip you have taken or would like to take. Tell what you did or will do. Tell what you saw or will see. Underline the predicate in each sentence.

Let's Talk About
EXPLORATION

Words to Read

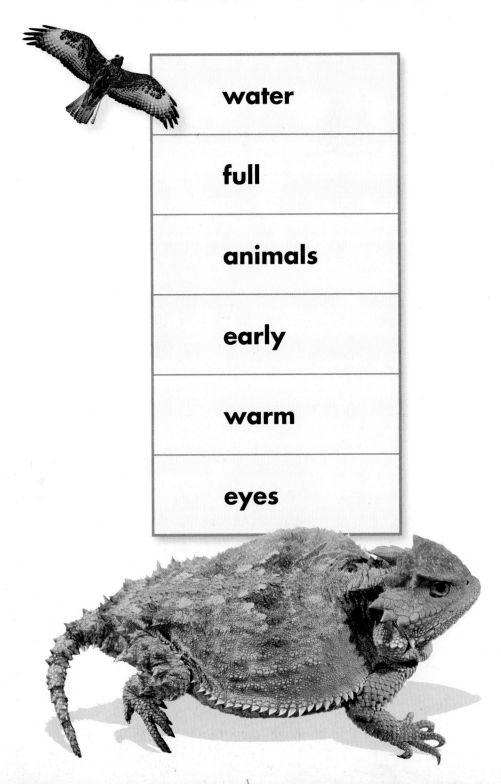

water
full
animals
early
warm
eyes

Read the Words

Some places on Earth have very little water. It is hot and dry, but these places are full of life. Plants and animals can live there. You can visit these places too. Go out early before the sun is too warm. Be sure to protect your eyes when you go out!

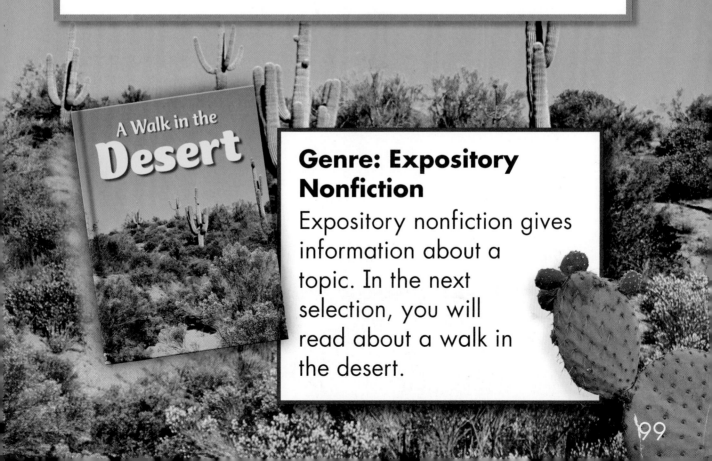

A Walk in the Desert

Genre: Expository Nonfiction

Expository nonfiction gives information about a topic. In the next selection, you will read about a walk in the desert.

A Walk in the Desert

by Caroline Arnold

What can you find on a walk in the desert?

101

See the bright sun. Feel the dry air. It is hot—very hot! Where are we?

We're in the desert. Let's take a walk and see what we can find.

The ground is dry in the desert. It almost never rains. With so little water, it is hard for anything to live. But many plants and animals make their home in this harsh climate. You just have to look closely to see them.

Teddy-Bear Cholla Cactus

Hedgehog Cactus

Cactus is one kind of plant that grows in the desert. It doesn't have leaves. Instead, it has sharp spines. The spines protect the cactus from animals who might want to eat it. A cactus stores water in its stem. It uses the water when there is no rain.

Prickly Pear Cactus

Barrel Cactus

Saguaro Cactus

Look up at the tall saguaro. It is a giant among cactus plants. It took many years to grow so tall.

In late spring, white flowers bloom. Birds and insects drink the flowers' sweet nectar. After the flowers die, a red fruit grows.

Prickly Pear Fruit

Saguaro Cactus with White Flowers

105

Hawk

Woodpecker

The saguaro cactus is home to many desert creatures. *Tap, tap, tap,* pecks a woodpecker. It is carving a hole for its nest. Old holes become nests for other birds.

A hawk is searching for food below. Its sharp eyes can spot even a tiny mouse.

Owl

What is that large bird? It's a roadrunner.
Coo, coo, coo, it calls. The roadrunner hardly
ever flies, but it can run fast. Watch it chase
a lizard to eat.

Roadrunner

Tree Lizard

Here are some other lizards. Lizards need the sun's heat to warm their scaly bodies. But when it gets too hot, they look for shade.

Zebra-Tailed Lizard

Leopard Lizard

Short-Horned Lizard

A rattlesnake lies next to a rock. Its earth colors make it hard to see. Rattlesnakes are dangerous. A bite from one will kill a small animal. If you hear a rattlesnake shake its tail, it is trying to scare you away.

Look! Did you see that rock move? It isn't a rock at all. It's a desert tortoise. The hard shell protects the tortoise from enemies and from the hot sun. The tortoise uses its sharp beak to break off tough desert grasses. It sometimes eats cactus fruits, too.

Rattlesnake

Cactus Fruits

Desert Tortoise

112

The jack rabbit is also a plant eater. Watch it sniff the early evening air. It is alert to the sounds and smells of the desert. When danger is near, the jack rabbit's long legs help it to escape quickly.

Jack Rabbits

As night begins to fall, the desert air cools. Animals who were hidden or sleeping come out to hunt and feed. A hungry coyote howls to the moon.

Do you see the small kit fox? Big ears help the fox to hear well so it can track animals to eat.

The cool night is full of activity.

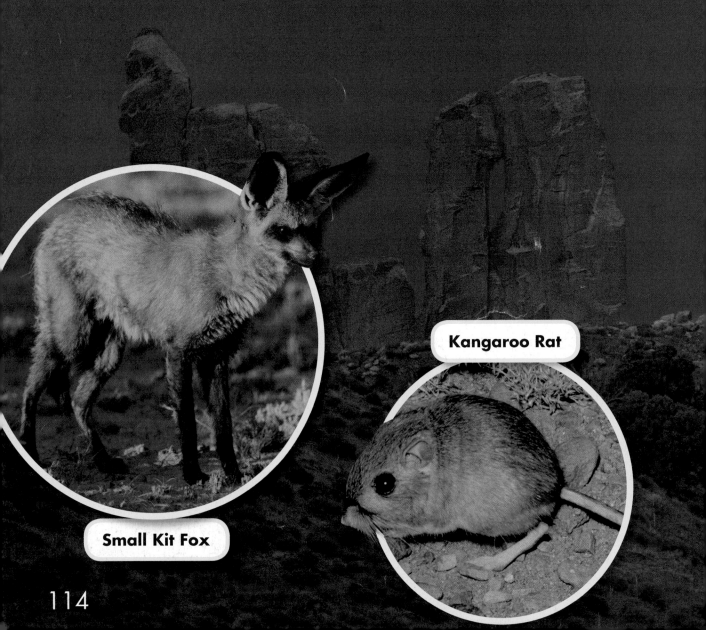

Kangaroo Rat

Small Kit Fox

Owl

Coyote

The desert is an exciting place to visit. You can ride a mule along a deep canyon, slide down a sand dune, learn about wildlife at a nature center, or taste sweet jelly made from prickly pear fruit.

Prickly Pear Fruit

Riding a mule

Sliding down a sand dune

117

You can find deserts all over the world. Not all deserts are alike. Some are hot. Others are cold. But in all deserts there is little rain.

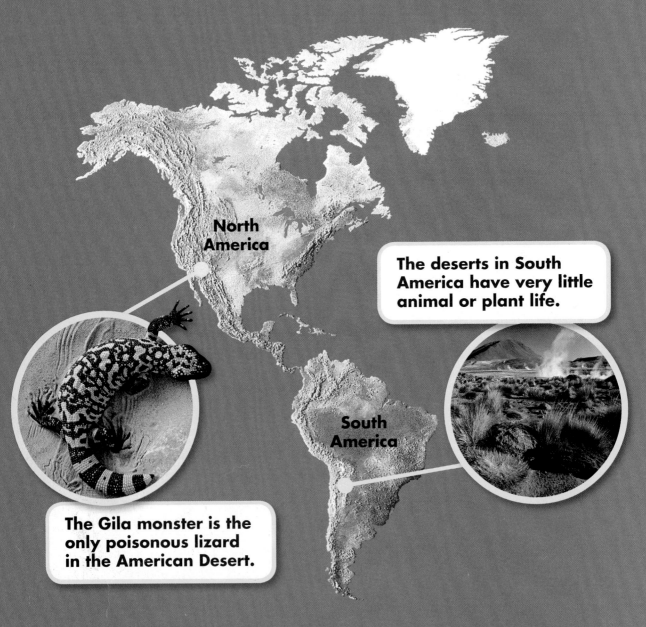

North America

The deserts in South America have very little animal or plant life.

South America

The Gila monster is the only poisonous lizard in the American Desert.

The Gobi desert is cold and snowy in the winter. Temperatures are often below freezing.

The tiny fennec fox lives in the world's largest desert—the Sahara.

Asia

Europe

Africa

The Australian Desert is home to the bandicoot.

Australia

The dromedary is a one-humped camel found in the sandy Arabian Desert.

Can you find the continent where you live?
Is there a desert on it?

Think and Share

Talk About It You and some friends go walking in the desert. Tell your friends what to look at and listen for.

1. Use the pictures below to summarize what you learned.

2. Look back at the story to find details that tell about desert plants and animals.

3. The author wrote about the desert as if she were taking you for a walk. Find examples of that in the selection. How did that help you as you read?

Test Practice

Look Back and Write Look at pages 116–117. What other things can you do in the desert?

Meet the Author
Caroline Arnold

Caroline Arnold has walked in several deserts in the southwestern United States. After she moved to California, she says, "I grew to love the desert."

Read two other books by Caroline Arnold.

Ms. Arnold is fascinated by the way living things adapt to the extreme heat and cold and the lack of water in the desert. "I get a thrill out of watching birds, squirrels, rabbits, coyotes, peccaries, lizards and other desert animals when I spend time in the desert," she says.

Rain Forests

Sammy read *A Walk in the Desert* and learned a lot. However, he knows that deserts are not everywhere. In fact, his home is near a forest. His family often goes there to fish, swim, and picnic. "But what exactly is a forest?" Sammy asks himself. To find out more, he goes to an online reference Web site.

Here Sammy finds four different sources: an atlas, an almanac, a dictionary, and an encyclopedia. Sammy clicks on Encyclopedia. Then he types the keyword *forest* into the search engine and clicks on "go." He gets a list of results that begins like this:

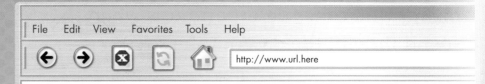

File   Edit   View   Favorites   Tools   Help

http://www.url.here

● **Search Results: forest**

forest (encyclopedia)

forest, a dense growth of trees, together with other plants, covering a large area of land.

Sammy clicks on the forest link and finds an encyclopedia article. As he reads it, he finds a link to Types of Forests. This makes him curious. He clicks on Types of Forests and finds this information.

Types of Forests

You can find rain forests all over the world, including Central and South America and Central and West Africa. Parts of Asia and Australia also have rain forests. Rain forests get lots of rain every year—160–400 inches. The average temperature is 80°F. Many different kinds of plants and animals live in rain forests.

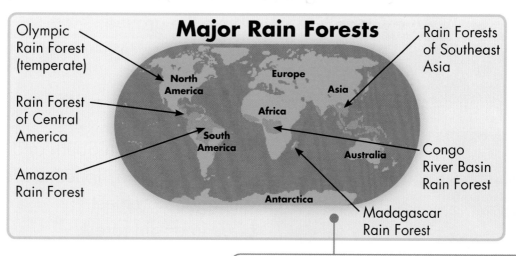

Major Rain Forests

Olympic Rain Forest (temperate)

Rain Forest of Central America

Amazon Rain Forest

Rain Forests of Southeast Asia

Congo River Basin Rain Forest

Madagascar Rain Forest

North America

Europe

Asia

Africa

South America

Australia

Antarctica

Sammy wonders where some of the countries with rain forests are. He uses the atlas on the Web site. He finds this map showing rain forests all over the world.

So far, Sammy has read part of an encyclopedia article and looked at a map. Sammy now goes back to the online reference Web site. He wants to find pictures of animals that live in rain forests. Sammy follows the steps and does another search. He finds these pictures on the Web site of a large university.

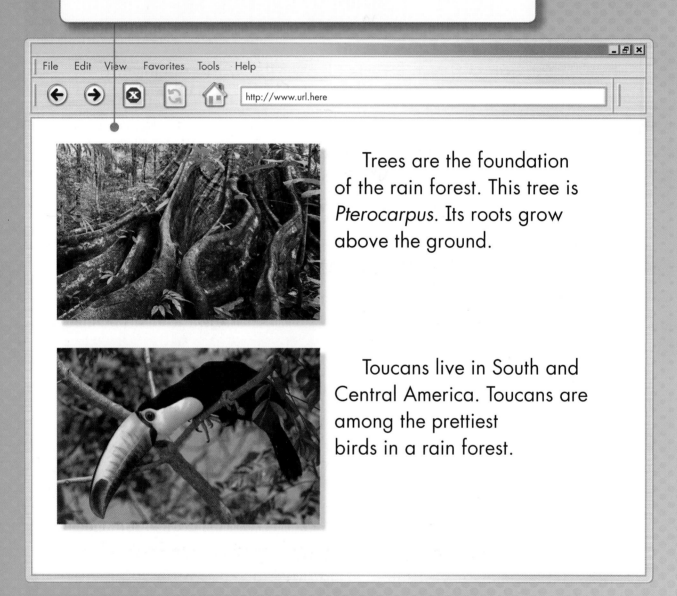

File   Edit   View   Favorites   Tools   Help

http://www.url.here

Trees are the foundation of the rain forest. This tree is *Pterocarpus*. Its roots grow above the ground.

Toucans live in South and Central America. Toucans are among the prettiest birds in a rain forest.

Some crocodiles grow to a very large size—up to twenty feet. But smaller ones (ten feet) are more usual.

Some native South Americans use the poison from poison dart frogs to make darts for hunting.

Sammy is so interested that he continues searching until he finds out all he needs to know about rain forests.

Statements and Questions

A **statement** is a sentence that tells something. A statement ends with a **period (.)**.

The desert is dry.

A **question** is a sentence that asks something. A question ends with a **question mark (?)**.

Do you see the small kit fox?

All statements and questions begin with capital letters.

Write Using Statements and Questions

1. Choose a statement and a question from the story. Write them. Circle the period and the question mark.

· ·

2. What else would you like to know about the desert? Write a question. Remember to begin your sentence correctly and to use a question mark at the end.

· ·

3. Imagine you are hiking in the desert. What would your day be like? Write some sentences about your day. Write at least one statement and one question.

Let's Talk About
Exploration

Words to Read

pieces
often
very
together
though
gone
learn

Read the Words

Chip looked at the pieces of the puzzle. He often did these things with his very best friend Mike. He and Mike couldn't work together today, though. Mike had gone to visit his uncle. Chip knew he would have to learn to do things on his own.

Genre: Play

A play is a story written to be acted out for others. Next, you will read a play about an ant who sets out to learn who is the strongest one.

The Strongest One

retold as a play by Joseph Bruchac
illustrated by David Diaz
from *Pushing Up the Sky*

What does Little Red Ant
learn about being strong?

Characters:

NARRATOR	MOUSE
LITTLE RED ANT	CAT
SECOND ANT	STICK
THIRD ANT	FIRE
FOURTH ANT	WATER
SNOW	DEER
SUN	ARROW
WIND	BIG ROCK
HOUSE	

Scene I: Inside the Ant's Hole

(On a darkened stage, the ants crouch together.)

NARRATOR: Little Red Ant lived in a hole under the Big Rock with all of its relatives. It often wondered about the world outside: Who in the world was the strongest one of all? One day in late spring Little Red Ant decided to find out.

LITTLE RED ANT: I am going to find out who is strongest. I am going to go outside and walk around.

SECOND ANT: Be careful! We ants are very small. Something might step on you.

THIRD ANT: Yes, we are the smallest and weakest ones of all.

FOURTH ANT: Be careful, it is dangerous out there!

LITTLE RED ANT: I will be careful. I will find out who is strongest. Maybe the strongest one can teach us how to be stronger.

Scene II: The Mesa

(Ant walks back and forth onstage.)

NARRATOR: So Little Red Ant went outside and began to walk around. But as Little Red Ant walked, the snow began to fall.

(Snow walks onstage.)

LITTLE RED ANT: Ah, my feet are cold. This snow makes everything freeze. Snow must be the strongest. I will ask. Snow, are you the strongest of all?

SNOW: No, I am not the strongest.

LITTLE RED ANT: Who is stronger than you?

SNOW: Sun is stronger. When Sun shines on me, I melt away. Here it comes!

(As Sun walks onstage, Snow hurries offstage.)

LITTLE RED ANT: Ah, Sun must be the strongest. I will ask. Sun, are you the strongest of all?

SUN: No, I am not the strongest.

LITTLE RED ANT: Who is stronger than you?

SUN: Wind is stronger. Wind blows the clouds across the sky and covers my face. Here it comes!

(As Wind comes onstage, Sun hurries offstage with face covered in hands.)

LITTLE RED ANT: Wind must be the strongest. I will ask. Wind, are you the strongest of all?

WIND: No, I am not the strongest.

LITTLE RED ANT: Who is stronger than you?

WIND: House is stronger. When I come to House, I cannot move it. I must go elsewhere. Here it comes!

(As House walks onstage, Wind hurries offstage.)

LITTLE RED ANT: House must be the strongest. I will ask. House, are you the strongest of all?

HOUSE: No, I am not the strongest.

LITTLE RED ANT: Who is stronger than you?

HOUSE: Mouse is stronger. Mouse comes and gnaws holes in me. Here it comes!

(As Mouse walks onstage, House hurries offstage.)

139

LITTLE RED ANT: Mouse must be the strongest. I will ask. Mouse, are you the strongest of all?

MOUSE: No, I am not the strongest.

LITTLE RED ANT: Who is stronger than you?

MOUSE: Cat is stronger. Cat chases me, and if Cat catches me, Cat will eat me. Here it comes!

(As Cat walks onstage, Mouse hurries offstage, squeaking.)

LITTLE RED ANT: Cat must be the strongest. I will ask. Cat, are you the strongest of all?

CAT: No, I am not the strongest.

LITTLE RED ANT: Fire must be the strongest.
I will ask. Fire, are you the strongest of all?

FIRE: No, I am not the strongest.

LITTLE RED ANT: Who is stronger than you?

FIRE: Water is stronger. When Water is poured on me, it kills me. Here it comes!

(As Water walks onstage, Fire hurries offstage.)

LITTLE RED ANT: Water must be the strongest.
I will ask. Water, are you the strongest of all?

WATER: No, I am not the strongest.

LITTLE RED ANT: Who is stronger than you?

WATER: Deer is stronger. When Deer comes, Deer drinks me. Here it comes!

(As Deer walks onstage, Water hurries offstage.)

LITTLE RED ANT: Deer must be the strongest. I will ask. Deer, are you the strongest of all?

DEER: No, I am not the strongest.

LITTLE RED ANT: Who is stronger than you?

DEER: Arrow is stronger. When Arrow strikes me, it can kill me. Here it comes!

(As Arrow walks onstage, Deer runs offstage with leaping bounds.)

LITTLE RED ANT: Arrow must be the strongest. I will ask. Arrow, are you the strongest of all?

ARROW: No, I am not the strongest.

LITTLE RED ANT: Who is stronger than you?

ARROW: Big Rock is stronger. When I am shot from the bow and I hit Big Rock, Big Rock breaks me.

LITTLE RED ANT: Do you mean the same Big Rock where the Red Ants live?

ARROW: Yes, that is Big Rock. Here it comes!

(As Big Rock walks onstage, Arrow runs offstage.)

LITTLE RED ANT: Big Rock must be the strongest. I will ask. Big Rock, are you the strongest of all?

BIG ROCK: No, I am not the strongest.

LITTLE RED ANT: Who is stronger than you?

BIG ROCK: You are stronger. Every day you and the other Red Ants come and carry little pieces of me away. Someday I will be gone.

Scene III: The Ant's Hole

NARRATOR: So Little Red Ant went back home and spoke to the ant people.

(The ants crouch together on the darkened stage.)

SECOND ANT: Little Red Ant has returned.

THIRD ANT: He has come back alive!

FOURTH ANT: Tell us about what you have learned. Who is the strongest of all?

LITTLE RED ANT: I have learned that everything is stronger than something else. And even though we ants are small, in some ways we are the strongest of all.

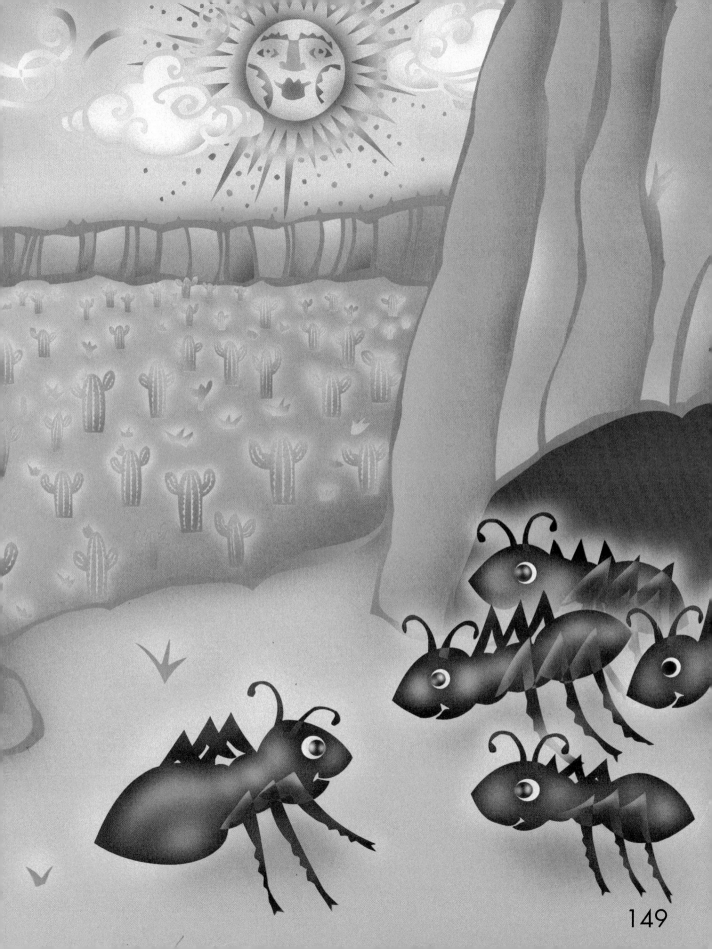

149

Think and Share

Talk About It You could do this play as a dance or a puppet show. Tell how.

1. Use the pictures below to retell the story. On another piece of paper, draw more pictures to show the missing parts.

2. Is *The Strongest One* a realistic story or a fantasy? What makes it so?

3. How is a play different from other selections? How did that change the way you read it?

Look Back and Write Look back at page 135. Why does Little Red Ant want to find the strongest one? Use details from the selection in your answer.

Meet the Author
Joseph Bruchac

As a child, Joseph Bruchac loved to explore nature— the animals, birds, insects, and plants around him. His grandfather, an Abenaki Indian, taught him many things about nature.

Today, Mr. Bruchac tells traditional Native American stories. "In the Abenaki Indian tradition," he says, "there is a story connected to just about every bird, animal, and plant." One message in many of these tales is that all parts of nature are important. Even tiny ants can make a difference!

Read more books by Joseph Bruchac.

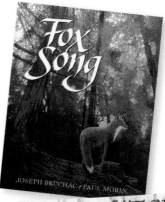

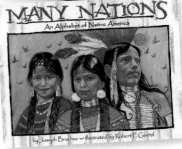

ANTEATERS

by John Jacobs

Have you ever heard of an anteater? Have you ever seen one? Let's learn more about them.

Central America

South America

Where do they live?

Anteaters live mostly in South and Central America where there are lots of grasses, swamps, and rain forests. These are the kinds of places where many ants live. Anteaters explore these grasses, swamps, and rain forests all day looking for ants to eat.

153

What do they look like?

The giant anteater, which is the most common, looks like nothing you've ever seen before. It has a bushy tail and a fat body. It has a tiny mouth, small eyes, and small ears. Its most important body parts are its sharp claws and its long, long tongue. (Its tongue is almost two feet long. That's as long as two rulers put together!)

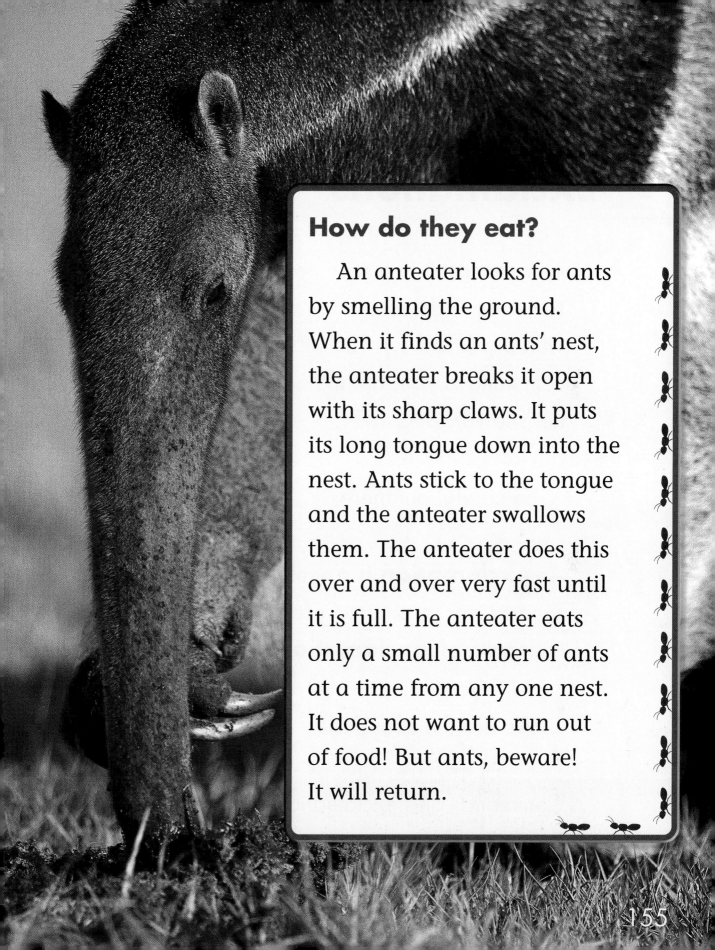

How do they eat?

An anteater looks for ants by smelling the ground. When it finds an ants' nest, the anteater breaks it open with its sharp claws. It puts its long tongue down into the nest. Ants stick to the tongue and the anteater swallows them. The anteater does this over and over very fast until it is full. The anteater eats only a small number of ants at a time from any one nest. It does not want to run out of food! But ants, beware! It will return.

Commands and Exclamations

A **command** is a sentence that tells someone to do something. It ends with a **period (.)**. The subject of a command is you, but the word *you* is not shown.

Be careful out there.

An **exclamation** is a sentence that shows surprise or strong feelings. It ends with an **exclamation mark (!)**.

We are the strongest!

Commands and exclamations begin with capital letters.

Write Using Commands and Exclamations

1. Write a sentence from the story that is an exclamation. Circle the exclamation mark.

. . . .

2. What would you have said to Little Red Ant about being strong? Write at least one command and one exclamation.

. . . .

3. If you were an ant, what other things would you want Little Red Ant to find out? Write some sentences. Write at least one command and one exclamation.

157

Wrap-Up

A Postcard from My Explorations

Which place did you read about that you would most like to explore? Imagine that you are there. Write a postcard to a friend. Tell about what you learned from exploring this place. Add a picture to your postcard.

It's amazing! The country is so different from the city. I didn't like it at first.

What can we learn from exploring new places and things?

The Strongest One

connect to

SCIENCE

In *The Strongest One*, an ant discovers that it, too, is strong. Think about things in nature. Are some things stronger than others? Make a list. Include yourself on the list. Put the list in order, from the strongest to the weakest. Then make a graph with pictures and labels. Show the strongest, the weakest, and everything in between.

| weakest |————————| strongest |

sun
me
rain
squirrel
dog
bee
snow

Comparing Surroundings

connect to

SOCIAL STUDIES

In this unit, you read about many different places that people can explore. Choose two places that are very different. Make a Venn diagram. Tell how the places are different. Tell how they are alike.

Big Bear / Both / The Desert

lake
bears
deer
trees

cactus
rattlesnakes
coyote
sand
canyon

159

Working Together

How can we work together?

Read It
ONLINE
sfsuccessnet.com

Tara and Tiree, Fearless Friends

connect to SOCIAL STUDIES

Faithful pets work together to save a life.

Narrative Nonfiction

Ronald Morgan Goes to Bat

connect to SOCIAL STUDIES

Ronald provides his team with spirit.

Realistic Fiction

Turtle's Race with Beaver

connect to SCIENCE

Beaver learns the importance of cooperation.

Folk Tale

The Bremen Town Musicians

connect to SCIENCE

Animals work together to stop the robbers.

Fairy Tale

A Turkey for Thanksgiving

connect to SOCIAL STUDIES

The animals work together to make a happy Thanksgiving.

Animal Fantasy

Let's Talk About
Working Together

Words to Read

family
pull
listen
once
heard
break

Read the Words

Tag is our family pet. He is a good dog. He will pull on my pants leg until I take him for a walk. He will listen and do what I say. Once he heard me call and came running so fast that I thought he would break a leg.

Genre: Narrative Nonfiction
Narrative nonfiction tells the story of a true event. Next you will read a true story about two dogs that saved their owner.

Tara and Tiree,
Fearless Friends

by Andrew Clements
illustrated by Scott Gustafson

What makes Tara and Tiree fearless friends?

When Jim was a boy in Canada, his family had dogs. Jim loved those dogs. They were like part of his family.

When Jim grew up, he still loved dogs. He learned how to train them. He helped dogs learn to be good.

He always said, "There is no such thing as a bad dog." Training dogs became Jim's job.

Jim had two dogs named Tara and Tiree.
Tara was mostly black. Tiree was mostly gold.
Jim loved them both, and they loved him, too.
Jim and his dogs liked the winter time.

They had good coats to keep warm. They
played in the snow. They went for long walks.

They liked going out, but they liked going back
in, too. It was good to sit by the fire and listen to
the wind.

Jim's house was by a lake. Every winter there was ice on it. One day Jim went for a walk out on the lake. Tara and Tiree went too. The dogs loved to run across the ice.

It was very cold. Jim was ready to go back home. Then all at once the ice broke. Jim fell into the cold, cold water.

Jim called for help. No one was near. No one could hear him. But Tara and Tiree heard Jim and came running. Jim wanted the dogs to stay away. He was afraid for them.

But Tiree loved Jim. She wanted to help.
When she came near the hole, the ice broke again.
Tiree fell into the water with Jim.

The water was so cold. Jim knew he did not
have much time. Jim tried to help Tiree get out.
But the ice broke more and more.

Jim hoped Tara would run away. He did not want her to fall in the water too. But Tara did not run away. She wanted to help.

First Tara got down low. Then she came closer, little by little. The ice did not break.

Jim put out his hand. Tara got very close.
Then Jim got hold of Tara's collar. Jim held on.
Tara pulled back, but Jim was too big. He was
still in the cold water.

Then Tiree did something very smart. She walked on Jim's back—up and out of the water! Tiree was cold, but she was safe! Did she run off the ice? No. She loved Jim too much to run away.

Tiree got down on her belly like Tara. She got close to Jim. Jim held out his other hand. And he grabbed on to Tiree's collar!

The two dogs pulled back hard. They slipped, but they didn't stop. Slowly they pulled Jim up onto the ice. He was safe.

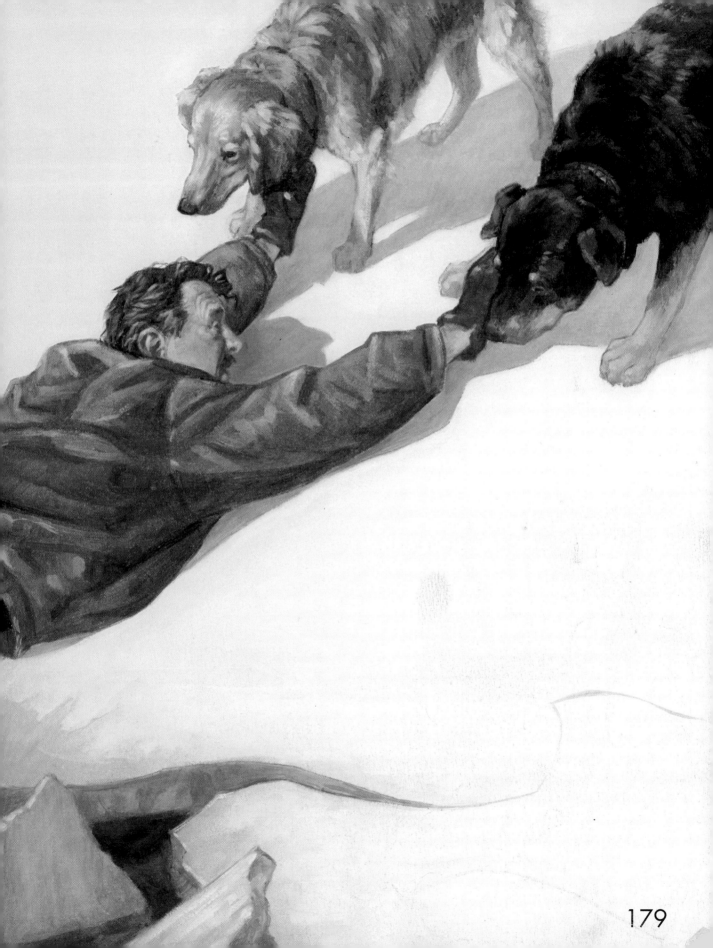

Tara and Tiree had saved his life! Soon they
were all back in the house. They sat by the fire
until they were warm again.

Jim always said, "There is no such thing as a
bad dog."

Now Jim says something else, too: "There *is* such a thing as a brave and wonderful dog!"

Jim is sure of this, because he has two of them—Tara and Tiree.

Think and Share

Talk About It Choose the most exciting part of this story. What makes it exciting? Read it.

1. Use the pictures below to retell the story.

2. Tara seemed to know what to do when Jim fell into the water. What did she do first? What happened next?

3. What did you predict would happen to Jim? Were you right? What other predictions did you make?

Look Back and Write Look back at pages 176 and 177. Tiree did something smart and something kind. What did she do? Use details from the selection in your answer.

Meet the Author

Andrew Clements

Andrew Clements says, "Every good writer I know started off as a good reader." When he was growing up, he loved to read. He remembers a school librarian who made him feel he was the "owner" of every book he read. He says, "That's one of the greatest things about reading a book—read it, and you own it forever."

Mr. Clements once taught school. Because he believes books make a difference, he read to his students in the classroom and to his four sons at home.

Read two more books by Andrew Clements.

Rescue Dogs

by Rena Moran

Do you know that dogs can be trained to save lives? These dogs are called rescue dogs. When people are in danger, rescue dogs are ready to help them.

Who do they help?

Rescue dogs find lost hikers and campers. They find people who are trapped after an earthquake or an avalanche. When people get lost in a snowstorm, rescue dogs search for them. Some dogs can even save people from drowning.

What kinds of dogs make good rescue dogs?

Good rescue dogs must be strong and smart. They also must listen to the people who train and handle them. Saint Bernards have been working as rescue dogs for many years. They help rescue people who get lost in snowstorms or get trapped under deep snow.

Bloodhounds, Labrador retrievers, and German shepherds are good at following the trails of lost people. German shepherds also are good at finding people who are trapped under snow. Newfoundlands do a great job with water rescues.

185

How do they do their jobs?

Like all dogs, rescue dogs have a very good sense of smell. They use their sense of smell to find a lost person. First, the dog sniffs something with the person's scent on it. This could be a hat or a blanket. Then, the dog follows the scent trail the person has left.

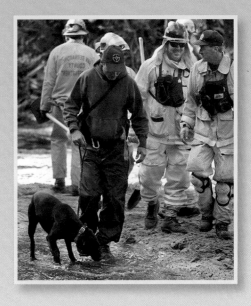

Rescue dogs do not always look for just one person. Often, they try to find the scent of any person in a certain spot. This is useful when more than one person is lost.

Of course, rescue dogs could not do their jobs without the people who train and handle them. Who are these people? Most of them are people who love working with dogs. They also like to help rescue people who are in danger— just like their dogs do!

Nouns

· ·

A **noun** names a person, place, animal, or thing.

· ·

The **boy** and his **dog** played with the **ball** in the **backyard.**

Boy names a person.

Dog names an animal.

Ball names a thing.

Backyard names a place.

Write **Using Nouns**

1. Choose a sentence from the selection. Write it. Underline the nouns.

· ·

2. Tara and Tiree are Jim's pets. Write a sentence about Tara and Tiree. Underline the nouns.

· ·

3. What would you teach a pet to do? Write some sentences telling about it. Underline the nouns in your sentences.

189

Let's Talk About
Working Together

Words to Read

you're

second

great

either

laugh

certainly

worst

Read the Words

You're invited to our second ball game of the year!

Come out and have a great time.

You will either laugh or cry, but you certainly will have fun.

We may have been the worst team last year, but this year will be our best ever!

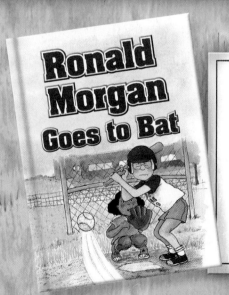

Genre: Realistic Fiction
Realistic fiction has made-up characters that act like real people. Read about Ronald Morgan, who is an important member of his baseball team.

Ronald Morgan

Goes to Bat

by Patricia Reilly Giff

illustrated by Susanna Natti

How can Ronald Morgan help his team?

Baseball started today. Mr. Spano said everyone could play.

"Even me?" I asked.

And Tom said, "You're letting Ronald Morgan play? He can't hit, he can't catch. He can't do anything."

Mr. Spano looked at me.

"Everyone," he said.

"Yahoo!" I yelled. I pulled on my red and white shirt, the one that says GO TEAM GO, and ran outside to the field.

"Two things," Mr. Spano told us. "Try hard, and keep your eye on the ball."

Then it was time to practice. Michael was up first. He smacked the ball with the bat. The ball flew across the field.

"Good," said Mr. Spano.

"Great, Slugger!" I yelled. "We'll win every game."

It was my turn next. I put on the helmet and stood at home plate.

"Ronald Morgan," said Rosemary. "You're holding the wrong end of the bat."

Quickly I turned it around. I clutched it close to the end.

Whoosh went the first ball.
Whoosh went the second one.
Wham went the third. It hit
me in the knee.

"Are you all right?" asked
Michael.

But I heard Tom say,
"I knew it. Ronald Morgan's
the worst."

At snack time, we told Miss Tyler about the team.

"I don't hit very well," I said.

And Rosemary said, "The ball hits him instead."

Everybody laughed, even me. I shook my head. "I hope it doesn't happen again."

Miss Tyler gave me some raisins. "You have to hit the ball before it hits you," she said.

We played every day. I tried hard, but the
ball came fast. I closed my eyes and swung.

"If only he could hit the ball once,"
Rosemary said.

And Billy shook his head.

I couldn't tell them I was afraid of the ball.
"Go, team, go," I whispered.

201

One day, the team sat on the grass.
We watched the third grade play. They
were big, they were strong, they were
good. Johnny hit a home run, and Joy
tagged a man out.

"We'll never hit like that," said Tom.

And Rosemary said, "We'll never catch like that either."

But I said, "Our team is the best."

Mr. Spano nodded. "That's the spirit, Ronald."

Mr. Spano told us, "Now we'll run the bases. Rosemary, you can go first."

Rosemary went fast. She raced for first base.

"Terrific, Speedy!" I yelled.

"Let me go next," I said. "I can do
that, too."

But the field was muddy. My sneaker
came off.

Jimmy said, "That kid's running bases
the wrong way."

And Tom yelled, "Ronald Morgan.
You're heading for third base."

The next day, we worked on catching.
I was out in left field. While I waited, I
found a stick, and started to scratch out
the mud. I wrote G for go. I wrote G for
great. Our team is the best, I thought.
Then I wrote H for hit. H for home run.
If only I could do that.

Just then I heard yelling. Someone had
hit the ball.

"Catch it, Ronald!" Tom shouted.

I put down the stick. I put up my mitt.
Too late. The ball sailed into the trees.

Mr. Spano took us for ice cream. "You
deserve it for trying," he said. "Our team is
really good."

I had a chocolate cone.

Michael's a slugger, I thought. And Rosemary can really run. But I'm still afraid of the ball.

On the way home, we saw some kids playing ball.

"Want to hit a few?" Michael asked.

I shook my head. "Maybe I won't play ball anymore."

Michael said, "We need you. You have spirit. You help the team feel good."

"But how can we win?" I asked. "I can't even hit the ball."

I saw my father and ran to catch up. "See you, Michael," I said.

My father asked, "How's the champ?"

"I'm the worst," I said.

"I was the worst, too," said my father. "But then. . . ."

"What?"

My father laughed. "I stopped closing my eyes when I swung."

"Maybe that's what I do."

"How about a little practice?" he asked.

We went into the yard. My father threw me some balls.

I missed the first one. . . . I missed the second. And then. . . . I opened my eyes and swung. *Crack* went the ball.

"Ouch!" went my father. "You hit me in the knee."

"Home run!" yelled my mother.

"Sorry," I said. "Hey, I did it!"

My father rubbed his knee. "You certainly did," he said.

I ran to pick up the ball. "See you later," I said.

My father smiled. "Where are you going?"

I grabbed the bat. "Some kids are
playing ball. I think I'll hit a few."

I looked back. "And you know
what else? I guess I'll stay on
the team. I have spirit . . . and
sometimes I can hit the ball. Mike
was right. I think they need me."

211

Think and Share

Talk About It What would you say to Ronald Morgan to help him play baseball?

1. Use the pictures below to retell the story. Tell what might come after the last picture. Draw a picture.

2. Is *Ronald Morgan Goes to Bat* a realistic story or a fantasy? How do you know?

3. What do you know about playing sports? How did that help you as you read?

Look Back and Write Look back at page 209. What did Ronald's father say that was helpful? Why was it helpful? Use information from the selection to support your answer.

Meet the Author
Patricia Reilly Giff

Books are important to Patricia Reilly Giff. She says, "While the rest of the kids were playing hide and seek, I sat under the cherry tree reading." She also says, "I wanted to write—always."

Ms. Giff got married, had three children, and taught school. Then she decided to follow her dream. She began writing. Some books come from her experiences. Others come from stories students told her.

Read more books by Patricia Reilly Giff.

Spaceball

by Brod Bagert

illustrated by Tedd Arnold

Last night I had a funny dream—
My brain's a mysterious place.
I dreamed about some aliens
Who lived in outer space.

I watched them play a game
That seemed a lot like baseball.
They played with bats and floppy hats,
But the aliens called it Spaceball.

Jupiter was the pitcher's mound,
Saturn was third base,
And the little alien kid at bat
Had a serious look on his face.

"Full count, bottom of the ninth,"
I heard the announcer say.
"This batter's trying to hit the ball
Clean out of the Milky Way."

Then I saw the ball was planet Earth!
Oh, how could it possibly be?
If he hits *that* ball, it's the end of us all,
That means . . . THE END OF ME!

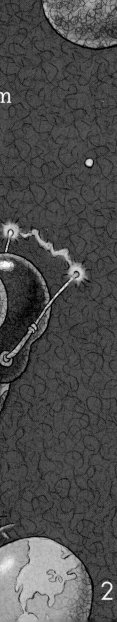

I heard a shout: "STRIKE THREE, YOU'RE OUT!"
And space was filled with cheers.
But the little alien batter's eyes
Filled up with alien tears.

My dreams are strange, but last night's dream
Was the strangest dream of all.
Earth was saved by an alien
Who couldn't hit the ball.

215

Proper Nouns

Proper nouns are special names for people, places, animals, and things. They begin with capital letters.

Ronald took his dog **Tramp** to **Fisher Park**.

Days of the week, months of the year, and **holidays** also begin with capital letters.

We played a ball game on **Memorial Day,** the fourth **Monday** in **May**.

Titles for people begin with capital letters. Many titles end with a **period (.)**.

Our coach, **Mr.** Morgan, taught us to throw the ball.

216

Write Using Proper Nouns

1. Write a sentence from the story that has more than one proper noun. Underline the proper nouns.

• •

2. Write a sentence about Ronald Morgan and his friends. Use proper nouns in your sentence. Underline the proper nouns.

• •

3. Write some sentences about a game you like to play at school or at home. Tell the name of the game. Tell when and where you play it. Tell how you play it. Underline the proper nouns in each sentence.

Let's Talk About
Working Together

Words to Read

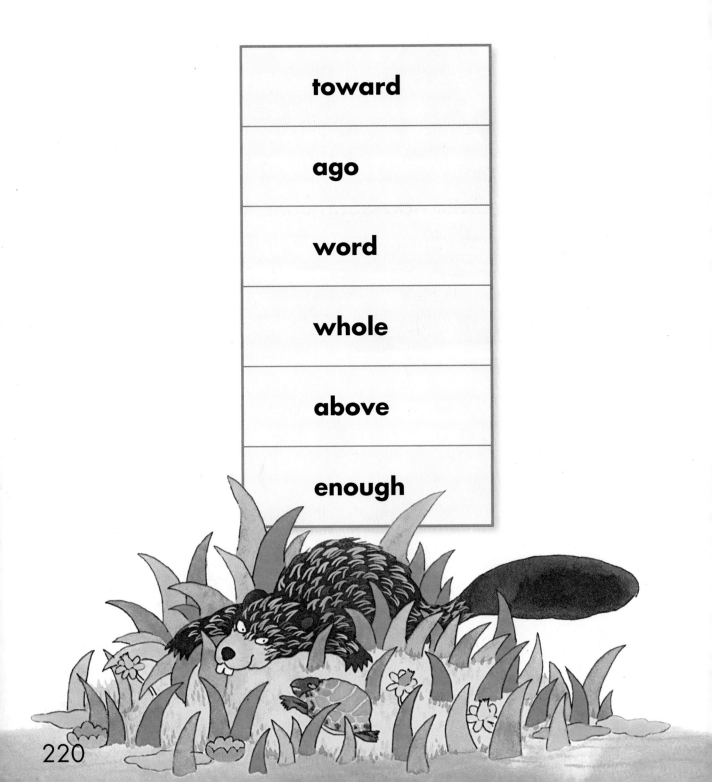

toward
ago
word
whole
above
enough

Read the Words

Beaver walked slowly toward the finish line. He had lost the race. Grandfather had told him long ago to always do his best. Beaver gave his word that he would. The whole forest had been cheering for him, but Turtle had won. Above all, Beaver had disappointed Grandfather. "Enough," Beaver told himself. "I will be a good sport and be happy for Turtle."

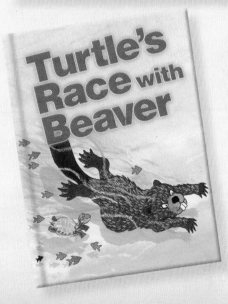

Genre: Folk Tale

A folk tale is a story that has been handed down from one generation to the next. Now you will read about Turtle and Beaver, who work out a problem by having a race.

Turtle's Race with Beaver

as told by Joseph Bruchac and James Bruchac
illustrated by Jose Aruego and Ariane Dewey

Why are Turtle and Beaver racing, and who will win?

Long ago, Turtle lived in a beautiful little pond.

She was very happy because this pond had everything a turtle needed. The water was just deep enough, there was plenty of food to eat, and there were lots of nice rocks just above the water for Turtle to sun herself on.

One day, as happens every year in the north, winter began to come to the land. As she had done year after year, Turtle swam to the bottom of the pond and buried herself in the thick mud.

While Turtle slept for the winter, another animal came walking along. It was Beaver, who had been looking for a new home.

"This will be perfect," said Beaver, "once I make some changes."

Soon he began doing one of the things beavers do so well. *Chomp! Chomp!* went Beaver as he took down one tree after another to build a big dam.

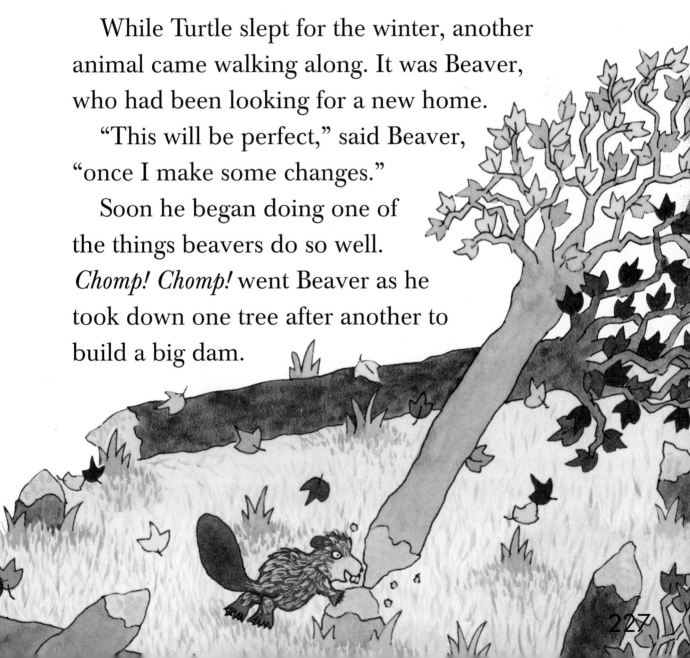

He worked hard for many days. And as he did, the water got deeper and deeper.

After finishing his dam, Beaver made himself a fine lodge of mud and sticks, then settled in for the rest of the winter. He was very happy.

The moons came and went, and spring returned once more to the land. The birds sang and the ice melted away. Then Turtle woke up. Crawling out from under the mud, she began to swim toward the surface of the water. But she had to swim higher, and higher, and higher, and higher.

By the time Turtle made it to the surface, she
realized that the water was four times as deep
as before! Her pond didn't look the same at all.
All of the rocks she loved to sun herself on were
under water. On one side the pond stretched
as far as her eyes could see. On the other stood
a huge dam. Not too far from that was a big
round lodge.

Then Turtle heard a loud *Whack!* She turned to see where the sound had come from. A strange animal was swimming toward her. It was Beaver.

"Who are you?" asked Beaver. "What are you doing here?"

"I am Turtle," Turtle said. "This is my pond. I have lived here my whole life."

"*Your* pond!" said Beaver. "This is *my* pond! Look at my wonderful dam and my splendid lodge. This is a beaver's pond."

"Yes," Turtle said, "I can see that you've done lots of work. Couldn't we just share the pond? There's plenty of room."

"Ha!" Beaver laughed. "I will not share my pond with any little turtle. But I *will* challenge you to a race. Whoever wins can stay, whoever loses must go find a new home."

Turtle didn't really want to race. She could see that Beaver, with his big flat tail, was probably a much faster swimmer. But this pond was the only home she knew.

"I agree," Turtle said. "We will race."

It was decided that the race would take place the next morning at first light. The two would meet on one side of the pond and race to the other.

That night, Beaver told other animals about the race. Word began to spread throughout the forest.

Squirrel told Rabbit, Rabbit told Fox, Fox told Wolf, Wolf told Deer, Deer told Moose, Moose told Bear. Soon every animal in the forest knew.

Before first light came to the land, all of the animals of the forest gathered around the pond. As they waited for Turtle and Beaver to arrive, many chose sides. Most of the smaller animals, such as Mouse, Chipmunk, and Rabbit, sided with Turtle. Most of the bigger animals, such as Wolf, Moose, and Bear, sided with Beaver.

As they waited, they began to sing:
TURTLE! BEAVER! TURTLE!
BEAVER! TURTLE! BEAVER!

They sang even louder when Beaver came swimming over from his lodge and Turtle popped up from under the water.
TURTLE! BEAVER! TURTLE! BEAVER! TURTLE! BEAVER!

Turtle and Beaver took their positions on the shore.

Bear lifted his big paw in the air.
"On your mark. . . get set. . . **GO!**"

SPLASH! went Beaver, leaping off from the shore.

He was certain he would leave Turtle far
behind. But Turtle had gotten an idea. Before
Beaver hit the water, Turtle stretched out her long
neck, opened her mouth, and bit into the end of
Beaver's tail.

FLAP! FLAP! FLAP! went Beaver, swimming as
fast as he could. But as fast as he went, Turtle was
right behind, holding on as hard as she could.

The other animals kept cheering, but now
some of the bigger animals were cheering for
Turtle instead of Beaver.

TURTLE! BEAVER! TURTLE!
BEAVER! TURTLE! *TURTLE!*

Soon Beaver was halfway across the pond. Even though Turtle was still holding on, it looked as if Beaver would win for sure. Then Turtle bit a little harder into Beaver's tail.

FLAP! FLAP! FLAP! Beaver swam even faster. Turtle still held on. Now more of the animals were cheering for Turtle.

TURTLE! BEAVER! TURTLE!
TURTLE! TURTLE! TURTLE!

Now they were almost to the other side. Beaver seemed sure to win. But Turtle bit as hard as she could into Beaver's tail. *CRUNCH!*

"*YEEEE-OWWWW!*" yelled Beaver. He flipped his big flat tail up and out of the water. When his tail reached its highest point, Turtle let go.

"Weeee!" sang Turtle as she flew through the air right over Beaver's head.

KA-THUNK! Turtle landed on the far shore and crawled across the finish line. Turtle had won the race. All the animals cheered.

TURTLE! TURTLE! TURTLE!
TURTLE! TURTLE! TURTLE!

Turtle was very pleased. But she could see how sad Beaver was. "I would still be happy to share my pond," she said.

But Beaver was so embarrassed that he left without another word.

Over time Beaver's dam fell apart and the water got shallower and shallower. Turtle had back all her wonderful rocks to sun herself on.

As for Beaver, he did find a new home in a pond not too far away. In that pond, though, there also lived a turtle.

"Can I share your pond with you?" Beaver asked.

"Of course," that other turtle said.

And so the two of them lived there happily
through all the seasons to come.

Think and Share

Talk About It What lesson did Beaver learn? How would you explain the lesson to a friend?

1. The pictures below show what happened at the beginning of the story. Tell what happened in the middle and at the end.

2. What was your favorite part of this story? What happened before and after that part?

3. Think about the race. How did it go? Summarize the part about the race.

Look Back and Write Look back at pages 241 and 242. Did Beaver learn a lesson? How do you know? Use details from the story in your answer.

Meet the Authors

Joseph and James Bruchac

Read more books by Joseph or James Bruchac.

Joseph Bruchac retells Native American stories to share with children. Mr. Bruchac says the best stories teach important lessons, but they also must be fun. Mr. Bruchac and his son James often write together.

James Bruchac says, "Stories about animals are by far my favorites. Our animal brothers and sisters are always teaching us things." James Bruchac is a wilderness expert. He runs the Ndakinna Wilderness Project in Greenfield Center, New York, where he teaches classes on animal tracking, hiking, and the natural world.

Meet the Illustrators

Jose Aruego and Ariane Dewey

Jose Aruego and Ariane Dewey have created pictures for more than seventy books. Usually Mr. Aruego draws the lines and Ms. Dewey paints the colors.

Read more books illustrated by these artists.

Jose Aruego grew up in the Philippines. His family had all sorts of animals, including pigs, horses, dogs, cats, and chickens. "Most of the characters in my books are animals. No matter how I draw them, they look funny," he says.

Ariane Dewey likes paddling a kayak and watching birds. Her favorite animals are turtles, butterflies, penguins, and polar bears.

THE SECRET LIFE OF
PONDS

by Elizabeth Schleichert
from *Ranger Rick*

Have you ever explored a pond? If so, you know how awesome these small, still bodies of fresh water can be. Most ponds aren't all that deep or wide. But they're definitely worth hanging out at!

To really see all the creatures living in one, you may need to get up close.

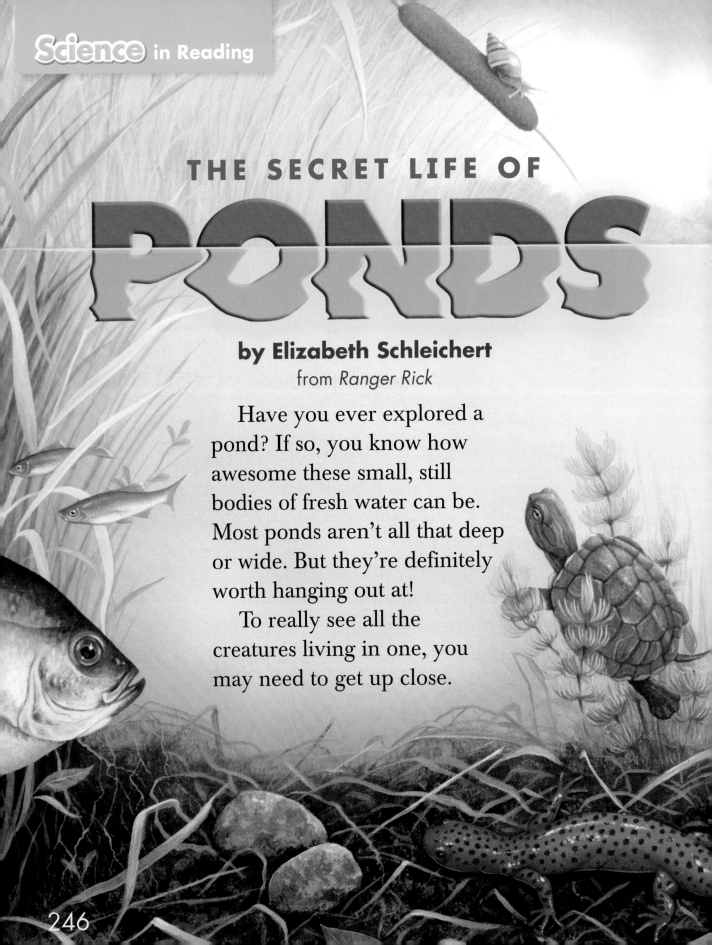

That's what this girl is doing. She is even wearing a swim mask to see all the creatures darting, diving, squiggling, crawling, and swimming down here. Snails, snakes, beetles, fish, tadpoles, and spiders—who knows what she's discovering?

Sometimes you can catch hints of what's living at a pond as you get near one. Maybe the quacking of geese or ducks alerts you to water up ahead! You hear a loud *"plunk"* as a frog or turtle hits the water. Or you listen to the noisy *kon-ka-ree* of red-winged blackbirds.

Along the pond's edge, you may see some tracks: Looks as if deer have come down for a drink. Foxes, raccoons, and skunks have poked around for a meal too. *Shhh!* Look over there! It's a great blue heron, wading in the water. It's waiting for a tasty fish or frog to come close enough for easy snatching.

Who knows what *you* might find at a pond? For some possibilities, just turn the page.

What's Here?

The painting shows a pond in the Midwest or Northeast. You might not see all of these plants and animals in one pond. But you'll most likely see some.

1. fragrant water lily
2. green frog
3. sunfish
4. cattail
5. damselflies
6. water scorpion
7. orb snail
8. pickerel
9. leech
10. red-spotted newt
11. dragonfly
12. whirligig beetles
13. red-eared slider
14. shiner
15. giant water bug
16. bullhead

248

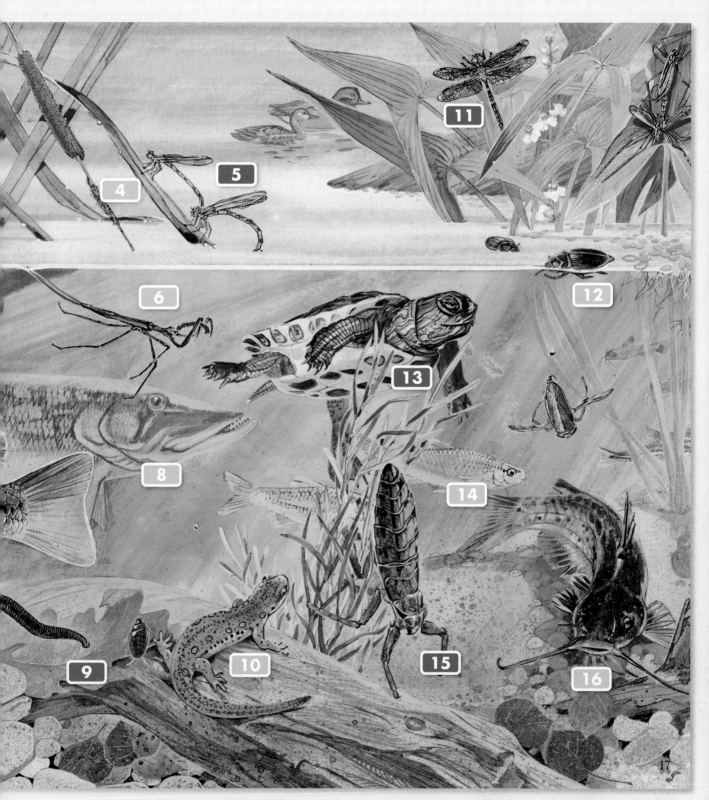

Singular and Plural Nouns

A **singular noun** names one person, place, animal, or thing.

Turtle rested on the **rock**.

A noun that names more than one is called a **plural noun**.

Turtle could not find any of her **rocks**.

You add **-s** to most nouns to show more than one. If a noun ends in **s, ch, sh,** or **x,** add **-es** to the noun to show more than one.

Two **foxes** watched the race from the **bushes**.

Write Using Singular and Plural Nouns

1. Find some singular nouns in the story. Make them plural. Write them.

2. Write a sentence to Beaver about why he should share the pond with Turtle. Use a singular and a plural noun. Underline them.

3. What food would you make for a picnic at the big race? Write how to make it. Use singular and plural nouns.

Let's Talk About
Working Together

Words to Read

| people |
| sign |
| bought |
| scared |
| probably |
| shall |
| pleasant |

Read the Words

People waited for hours to get tickets for the big concert. One man made a sign asking for extra tickets! Some wise fans bought their tickets months ago. They were scared by all the talk that the concert would probably be sold out.

"I shall do my best," one singer said. "I think this will be a very pleasant concert."

The Bremen Town Musicians

Genre: Fairy Tale
A fairy tale usually takes place long ago and far away and has fantastic characters. Next you will read about four animals that become friends and travel to a faraway town.

The Bremen Town Musicians

retold as a play by Carol Pugliano

illustrated by Jon Goodell

Who are the Bremen Town Musicians?

257

NARRATOR 1: Once there was a donkey. He worked hard for his owner for many years. Day after day he carried heavy bags of grain to the mill.

NARRATOR 2: But the donkey grew old. He could no longer work hard. One day he heard his owner talking about him. He said he was going to get rid of the donkey. The donkey was worried.

DONKEY: Oh, no! What will happen to me?
I must run away. I'll go to Bremen.
There I can be a fine musician.
(The donkey sings this song:)

Off I go to Bremen Town.
It's the place to be!
I will play my music there.
People will love me!
With a hee-haw here,
And a hee-haw there.
Here a hee, there a haw,
Everywhere a hee-haw.
Off I go to Bremen Town.
It's the place to be!

NARRATOR 1: So the donkey left that night. He had not gone far when he saw a dog lying on the ground.

NARRATOR 2: The dog looked weak. He also looked sad. The donkey knelt down to speak to the dog.

DONKEY: What is the matter, my friend?

DOG: Ah, me. Now that I am old and weak, I can no longer hunt. My owner wants to get rid of me. I got scared, so I ran away. Now I don't know what I will do.

DONKEY: You can come with me to Bremen. I am going to be a musician. Will you join me?

DOG: I'd love to! I can bark very pleasant tunes.

DOG AND DONKEY: Off we go to Bremen Town. It's the place to be! We will play our music there. We'll be filled with glee!

DONKEY: With a hee-haw here, and a hee-haw there. Here a hee, there a haw, everywhere a hee-haw.

DOG: With a bow-wow here and a bow-wow there. Here a bow, there a wow, everywhere a bow-wow.

DOG AND DONKEY:
Off we go to Bremen Town. It's the place to be!

261

NARRATOR 1: So, the donkey and the dog set off for Bremen. Soon, they saw a cat sitting by the road.

NARRATOR 2: The cat had the saddest face the donkey and the dog had ever seen. They stopped to find out what was wrong.

DOG: Hello there. Why so glum?

CAT: Ho, hum. Now that I am old and my teeth are not sharp, I cannot catch mice. My owner wants to get rid of me. I don't know what I will do.

DONKEY: You'll come to Bremen with us, that's what! We are going to become musicians. Won't you join us?

CAT: Sure I will! I love to meow.

DONKEY, DOG, AND CAT:
Off we go to Bremen Town.
It's the place to be!
We will play our music there.
We're a gifted three!

DONKEY: With a hee-haw here,
and a hee-haw there.
Here a hee, there a haw,
everywhere a hee-haw.

DOG: With a bow-wow here,
and a bow-wow there.
Here a bow, there a wow,
everywhere a bow-wow.

CAT: With a meow-meow here,
and a meow-meow there.
Here a meow, there a meow,
everywhere a meow-meow.

ALL: Off we go to Bremen Town.
It's the place to be!

NARRATOR 1: The three musicians walked along some more. They came to a farmyard. There they heard a rooster crowing sadly.

ROOSTER: Cock-a-doodle-doo! Cock-a-doodle-doo!

DONKEY: My, you sound so sad. What is wrong?

ROOSTER: I used to crow to wake up the farmer each morning. But he just bought an alarm clock. Now he doesn't need my crowing so he wants to get rid of me. Now I'm a cock-a-doodle-*don't!* Oh, what will I do?

DOG: Come with us to Bremen. We're going to be musicians.

CAT: With your fine crowing, we'll make a wonderful group!

ROOSTER: I cock-a-doodle-*do* think that's a wonderful idea! Let's go!

DONKEY, DOG, CAT, AND ROOSTER:

Off we go to Bremen Town. It's the place to be!
We will play our music there. We're a sight to see!

DONKEY: With a hee-haw here, and a hee-haw there.
Here a hee, there a haw, everywhere a hee-haw.

DOG: With a bow-wow here, and a bow-wow there.
Here a bow, there a wow, everywhere a bow-wow.

CAT: With a meow-meow here, and a meow-meow
there. Here a meow, there a meow, everywhere a
meow-meow.

ROOSTER: With a cock-a-doodle here, and a cock-a-doodle there. Here a doodle, there a doodle, everywhere a cock-a-doodle.

ALL: Off we go to Bremen Town. It's the place to be!

NARRATOR 2: The four musicians walked until it got dark. Finally, they saw a sign that said Bremen Town. They danced with excitement, but they were also very tired. They wanted to rest.

NARRATOR 1: They saw light coming from a little house up the road. They walked up to the window, but none of the animals were tall enough to see inside. So, the dog stood on the donkey's back, the cat stood on the dog's back, and the rooster stood on the cat's back and peeked inside.

DOG: What do you see, rooster?

ROOSTER: I think there are three robbers in there! They are sitting at a table full of delicious-looking food!

CAT: Food? I'm starving! What shall we do? We must get them out of that house!

ROOSTER: I have a plan. Listen closely.

NARRATOR 2: The rooster whispered his plan to the others.

NARRATOR 1: All of a sudden, the four began singing. They made quite a noise. When the robbers heard the animals, they ran out of the house screaming!

NARRATOR 2: The four musicians went inside the house. There they ate and ate until they were full. Then, it was time for bed.

269

NARRATOR 1: The donkey slept in the soft grass in the yard. The dog slept behind the front door. The cat slept near the warmth of the fireplace. And the rooster slept high on a bookshelf.

270

NARRATOR 2: After a while, the robbers returned to finish eating their feast.

ROBBER 1: That noise was probably just the wind. Besides, I can't wait to eat the rest of that roast beef!

ROBBER 2: I can taste those mashed potatoes now!

ROBBER 3: I'll go first just to make sure it's safe.

NARRATOR 1: So the robber went inside. He was cold, so he went to the fireplace to warm himself. There he surprised the cat, who scratched his face.

NARRATOR 2: The robber ran to the front door. The dog was startled and bit his leg. The robber ran outside. He tripped over the donkey, who kicked him.

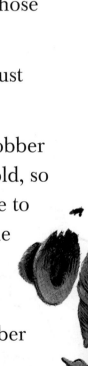

NARRATOR 1: All this noise woke the rooster up. He started screeching, "Cock-a-doodle-doo!" The robber ran back to his friends.

ROBBER 3: There are four horrible monsters in there! One scratched me with its long nails. Another bit me. Another kicked me. And the fourth one screamed, "Coming to get yooouuuuu!"

ROBBER 1: Four monsters! Let's get out of here!

NARRATOR 2: And the robbers ran off, never to be heard from again.

NARRATOR 1: But the four musicians stayed there. They sang every night in Bremen, where they became the famous Bremen Town Musicians!

Think and Share

Talk About It You have seen the Bremen Town Musicians perform. Tell about the show they put on for you.

1. Put the pictures below in order to tell the story of the Bremen Town Musicians.

2. What do you think the author is trying to tell us with this story?

3. This play has a beginning, middle, and end. The characters also have a problem. What is it and how is it solved?

Look Back and Write Why are the three robbers afraid of the animals? Look back at page 272. Use details from the story in your answer.

Meet the Author

Carol Pugliano-Martin

Here are two books by Carol Pugliano-Martin with plays you may want to perform.

Carol Pugliano-Martin has written many plays for schoolchildren to perform. Some of her plays are about real Americans. Others tell about the heroes of American folk tales. Ms. Pugliano-Martin lives in White Plains, New York.

Animals
Helping Animals

by Jacquelyn Siki

Did you know that some animals help one another? Sometimes they do this in unusual ways.

The sea animal that looks like a plant is called a *sea anemone*. The anemone will sting almost any fish that comes near it but not the clown fish. For some reason, the anemone does not hurt the clown fish. The clown fish can swim among the waving arms of the anemone and be safe from other fish that might try to hurt it.

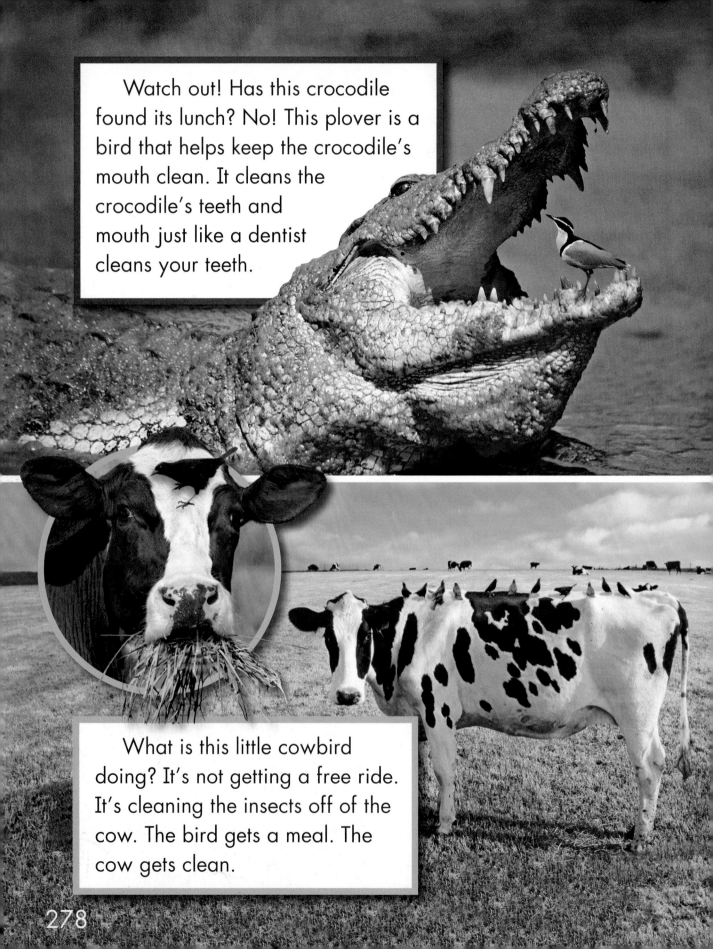

Watch out! Has this crocodile found its lunch? No! This plover is a bird that helps keep the crocodile's mouth clean. It cleans the crocodile's teeth and mouth just like a dentist cleans your teeth.

What is this little cowbird doing? It's not getting a free ride. It's cleaning the insects off of the cow. The bird gets a meal. The cow gets clean.

This bird, called a *honey guide*, leads a *ratel*, or honey badger, to a beehive. The honey guide likes honey, and so does the badger. But the honey guide needs the badger's help to break open the hive. Then both animals can enjoy a treat!

These animals help each other too. When they are at a water hole together, baboons and impalas warn one another of danger. Baboons will even try to drive the danger away!

Like people, many animals help one another. They do this so that they can live together and survive.

Plural Nouns That Change Spelling

A **plural noun** names more than one person, place, animal, or thing. Some nouns change spelling to name more than one.

Cat saw one **mouse** in the house.

Cat saw two **mice** by the door.

Singular	Plural
leaf	leaves
tooth	teeth
foot	feet
man	men
woman	women
goose	geese

Write Using Plural Nouns That Change Spelling

1. Write this sentence so that the singular noun *man* is plural.

The man heard the rooster crowing.

· ·

2. Choose an animal from the play. Write a sentence about that animal. Use a plural noun that changes spelling. Underline the plural noun.

· · · · · · · · · · · · · · · · · · · ·

3. Write some sentences telling the animals how to get to Bremen Town. Use plural nouns from the chart on page 280 in your sentences.

Let's Talk About
Working Together

Words to Read

| everybody |
| sorry |
| promise |
| minute |
| brought |
| behind |
| door |

Read the Words

It was the night before the big dinner. Everybody was coming—everybody but Sheep. Mr. Moose was sorry about that. But he made a promise to invite Sheep another time. Now Mr. Moose had to get busy. He didn't like to wait until the last minute to do anything. He brought in firewood from behind the door and began cooking. Soon the feast was ready.

Genre: Animal Fantasy
The animal characters in an animal fantasy act like people. Read about Mr. Moose and how he finds a turkey for Thanksgiving.

A Turkey for Thanksgiving

by Eve Bunting
illustrated by Diane de Groat

What will Mr. Moose do with a turkey for Thanksgiving?

It was Thanksgiving morning. Mr. Moose helped Mrs. Moose set the Thanksgiving table.

"Sheep will sit here. He likes a chair that's straight up and down," Mr. Moose said. "Rabbit here. Porcupine here. Mr. and Mrs. Goat here." He smiled at his wife. "Isn't it nice to have friends to share Thanksgiving?"

Mrs. Moose set two paper pilgrims, one at each end of the table. She placed the paper turkey with its great fan of a tail between the candles, and stood back.

"They look good, my dear," Mr. Moose said.

Mrs. Moose sighed. "Yes. But I wish we had a real turkey. Everyone always has a turkey for Thanksgiving. Everyone but us."

Mr. Moose nuzzled Mrs. Moose's head. "Well, that won't do. I will go this minute and find you a turkey for Thanksgiving."

Mr. Moose put on his cap and went out.

Mist wandered through the bare trees. The cold made his nose water.

Rabbit poked his head from his rabbit hole. "Mr. Moose! Is it dinnertime?"

"Not quite yet. Mrs. Moose wants a turkey. I'm off to find one."

Rabbit joined him in three quick hops. "I'll come, too."

Moose's warm breath hung white in front of him. Snow crunched under his hooves and made little holes that Rabbit jumped over.

"I see the Goats," Rabbit said.

Mr. Goat raised his head and spat out the tin can he was chewing. "Is it dinnertime?" he called.

"Not till I find a turkey," Mr. Moose said.

"We saw one down by the river," Mrs. Goat told him, and Mr. Goat added, "A fat one."

The Goats leaped down from their perch.
"We'll show you."

Sheep was farther up the hillside, looking round
as a fur ball in his winter coat. "Is it dinnertime?"
he bellowed.

"First I have to find a turkey," Mr. Moose
bellowed back.

"There's a turkey nest on the riverbank,"
Sheep called. "Wait for me."

The earth smelled of ice and moss as they crunched along. Above them a crow hung, black as a puff of wood smoke.

Porcupine was hiding in the underbrush.

"It's you," he said and put his quills down.

"We're off to get a turkey for Mrs. Moose," Mr. Moose explained. "Do you want to come?"

"I'm slow," Porcupine said. "Pick me up on your way back."

"Who'd want to pick you up?" Sheep asked, and laughed his bleat of a laugh.

"I'll wait," Porcupine told Mr. Moose.

They saw Turkey's nest right away, and Turkey himself peering over the top of it.

"Turkey! Turkey!" Mr. Moose called in his sweetest voice.

"Aagh!" Turkey blundered from his nest and ran.

Mr. Moose lumbered after him. "Turkey! Don't run. We just want you for Thanksgiving dinner."

Turkey ran faster.

Mr. Moose saw the red and blue sheen of Turkey's neck. Turkey's tail brushed crumbs of snow behind him as he tried to fly.

"Too fat," Mr. Goat said.

Turkey's legs bent in the middle as he fell.

Mr. Moose put a booted hoof on his head and smiled his great, toothy smile. "I hope you don't have other plans for Thanksgiving, Turkey."

He helped Turkey up. "My wife won't mind that you're too fat," he said. "Let's go. It's getting close to dinnertime."

They marched Turkey in front. "I'm sorry about this, for I can see you don't want to come," Mr. Moose said. "But I must insist. A promise is a promise."

There was a wreath of dried fruit on the Mooses'
door. Inside, the house was filled with Thanksgiving
smells. Mr. Moose hid Turkey behind him.

"Look who I brought, Mrs. Moose," he said.
"Sheep, the Goats, Rabbit, and Porcupine. And
ta-da!" He pushed Turkey around in front of him.
"For you. A turkey for Thanksgiving!"

Mrs. Moose clapped her hooves. "I'm *so* happy
to have you, Turkey. Thank you, Mr. Moose. Now
everything's perfect."

"Shall we sit?" Sheep asked, heading for the straight-up-and-down chair.

"Let's." Mrs. Moose pointed. "Rabbit here. Porcupine here. Mr. and Mrs. Goat here, and look! I brought a chair from the other room in hopes of Turkey."

"A . . . a *chair*?" Turkey stammered.

"Right next to me," Mrs. Moose said. "Light the candles, Mr. Moose."

There were bowls of acorns and alfalfa sprouts, dried since summer. There was willow bark and cured grasses and wild parsley. There were pressed leaves, thin and pale as new ice on a pond.

"I hope you find something here to your liking, Mr. Turkey," Mrs. Moose said. "I wasn't sure of your taste."

"You are so kind to worry about my taste," Turkey said. "I thought you'd be worrying about *how* I'd taste."

"Heavens, no!" Mr. Moose smiled his big-toothed smile and filled everyone's cup with cold spring water. "It's so nice to have friends around the table at Thanksgiving."

Turkey's wattles wobbled. "It's even nicer to be AT your table and not ON it," he said. "Happy Thanksgiving, everybody."

"Happy Thanksgiving, Turkey."

Think and Share

Talk About It Pretend you are Turkey. Tell why you are afraid to come to dinner.

1. The pictures below show the beginning, middle, and end of the story. Retell the story. Fill in the missing parts.

2. What conclusion did Turkey draw? Why would he think that?

3. Read page 295 again. What picture do you have in your mind as you read that page?

Look Back and Write Look back at page 300. Make a list of the foods Mrs. Moose served her guests. How do you think everyone enjoyed the dinner? What makes you think so?

Meet the Author
Eve Bunting

Read other books by Eve Bunting.

Eve Bunting does not eat turkey. She always thinks "poor turkey" when she sees a bird being put into the oven. That feeling is where she got the idea for *A Turkey for Thanksgiving*, one of her favorite books.

Ms. Bunting grew up in Ireland. There they do not celebrate a holiday like Thanksgiving.

Ms. Bunting loves to write. She has written over two hundred books for children. She has written about giants and ogres and creatures with scales and fins. She has written about sharks and whales and giant squid. She has written about children growing up and men growing old. Writing an animal fantasy like *A Turkey for Thanksgiving* is her "fun and relaxing time."

Meet the Illustrator
Diane de Groat

Diane de Groat has "a large picture file with photos of everything in the whole wide world." She used that file to help her draw the animals for *A Turkey for Thanksgiving*.

Read two more books illustrated by Diane de Groat.

She likes changing pictures of real animals into the characters in a story. "It's fun to choose what clothes they wear and what kind of expressions they should have." The turkeys were the hardest to draw. "They are not the most attractive birds, if you know what I mean."

Thanksgiving USA

After reading *A Turkey for Thanksgiving*, Nadia wants to learn more about the Thanksgiving holiday. With her parents' permission, Nadia searches the Web. She finds a Web site with many links.

Nadia clicks on one link, Thanksgiving. A new Web page opens. She finds these choices:

File   Edit   View   Favorites   Tools   Help

http://www.url.here

- **Search Results: thanksgiving**
- Thanksgiving USA

  Thanksgiving Canada

  Harvest Festival UK

Nadia chooses the link Thanksgiving USA. This link opens a new Web page.

Thanksgiving USA

In 1620 a ship, the Mayflower, sailed across the Atlantic Ocean. It was headed to America. About one hundred people were on this ship. The Pilgrims, as they were called, traveled to what is now Massachusetts. Their first winter was hard. They had come too late to plant and grow food. Without fresh food, half of the Pilgrims died.

The following spring, the Iroquois Indians showed the Pilgrims how to grow corn and other plants. The Indians showed the Pilgrims how to hunt and fish. By the fall of 1621, the Pilgrims had grown a lot of food. They had much to be thankful for. They planned a huge day for giving thanks. They invited the Indian chief and 90 Indians. The Indians brought deer to roast and other foods. The Indians had taught the Pilgrims different ways to cook corn and squash. The Indians even brought popcorn to this first Thanksgiving.

Nadia uses the scroll bar on the right-hand side of the Web page to find out more about Thanksgiving.

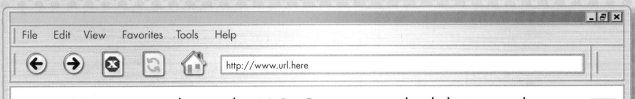

File   Edit   View   Favorites   Tools   Help

http://www.url.here

Many years later, the U.S. Congress asked that one day every year be set aside for the whole country to celebrate and give thanks. George Washington chose the date November 26 as Thanksgiving Day. Then in 1863, Abraham Lincoln asked all Americans to set aside the last Thursday in November as a day of thanksgiving.

Today, Thanksgiving falls on a different date every year, but it is always on the fourth Thursday of November.

Possessive Nouns

A noun that shows who or what owns something is a **possessive noun.** To show ownership, add an **apostrophe (')** and **-s** when the noun is singular. Add just an **apostrophe (')** when the noun is plural.

The quills of the **porcupine** are sharp.

The **porcupine's** quills are sharp.

The **'s** shows that the quills belong to one porcupine.

The house of the **goats** is by the river.
The **goats'** house is by the river.

The **'** after the **s** shows that the house belongs to more than one goat.

Write Using Possessive Nouns

1. Rewrite these phrases using possessive nouns.

the long ears of two rabbits

the feathers of one turkey

· ·

2. Write a sentence that tells about Turkey. Use possessive nouns to show ownership.

· ·

3. Who would you invite for Thanksgiving dinner? Write some sentences to use as an invitation. Use possessive nouns to show ownership.

Working Together Poster

connect to WRITING

Think about all the stories you read in this unit. What lessons did you learn from them? Work with a group. Make a list of rules for working together in school. Talk about what you learned from the stories as you make your list.

Rules for Working Together

1. _____

2. _____

3. _____

4. _____

5. _____

How can we work together?

Go Along, Get Along Sock Puppets

connect to
DRAMA

Choose two characters from different stories in Unit 2. Make a sock puppet for each one. Have the two puppets talk to each other. They should tell about what happened to them and what they learned about working together with others.

Team Member Award

connect to
SOCIAL STUDIES

Ronald Morgan was not a great hitter, but he was an important part of his team. Think about how you add something important to a group. Make an award for yourself. The award should show and tell about how you help the group as you work together.

Tony
the Reading helper
I help other kids read hard books.

Creative Ideas

What does it mean to be creative?

Read It
ONLINE
sfsuccessnet.com

Let's Talk About
Creative Ideas

Words to Read

shoe

science

village

guess

won

pretty

watch

Read the Words

"Pearl?" Wagner asked. "Did you ever find your shoe?"

"Yes," Pearl said. "I lost it at the science fair when you opened the ant village."

"I guess setting the ants free was a bad idea. I just wanted to win a prize."

"Well, nobody won because ants were everywhere," said Pearl. "It wasn't a pretty sight."

"I guess it's better to watch ants from the outside in," Wagner said.

"I guess it is," Pearl replied.

Genre: Animal Fantasy
In an animal fantasy, the animal characters act like humans. Next, you will read about Pearl and Wagner at the science fair.

Pearl and Wagner
Two Good Friends

by Kate McMullan · illustrated by R.W. Alley

Trash-eating Robot

New & improved

Look at the ANTS
The ants dig and dig and dig to make tunnels. It's a good life

The Robot

Everyone in Ms. Star's class was talking about the Science Fair.

"I am going to make a robot," said Pearl.

"I am going to win a prize," said Wagner.

Pearl got to work. She taped up the flaps
of a great big box. She cut a hole in the top.
Then she cut a hole in the lid of a shoe box.
She glued the shoe box lid to the top of the
great big box. Wagner held the boxes together
while the glue dried.

"Maybe I will make a walkie-talkie," he said.

Pearl punched a hole in one end of the
shoe box. She stuck string through the hole.
She tied the string in a knot.

"Maybe I will make a brain out of clay,"
said Wagner.

"Cool," said Pearl.

She drew eyes and a nose on the shoe box.
Wagner looked at the shoe box.

"The eyes are too small," he said.

Pearl made the eyes bigger.

"Maybe I will make a rocket," said Wagner.
"*Vrooom!* Blast off!"

Pearl put the shoe box onto the lid.

"There!" she said. "Finished!"
Pearl pulled the string.
The robot's mouth opened.
She threw in a wad of paper.
Then she let go of the string.
The robot's mouth shut.
"Wow!" said Wagner.
"A trash-eating robot!"

"Let's see what everyone has made," said Ms. Star.

"Uh-oh," said Wagner. He had not made anything yet.

Lulu raised her hand. "I made a walkie-talkie," she said.

"I was going to do that!" said Wagner.

"I made paper airplanes," said Bud. "This chart shows how far they flew."

Wagner slapped his head. "Why didn't *I* think of that?"

Henry showed how to get
electricity from a potato.

"Henry is a brain,"
said Pearl.

"Pearl?" Wagner said.
"Remember how I held
the boxes together
while the glue dried?"

"I remember," said Pearl.

"Remember how I told you
to give the robot bigger eyes?"
asked Wagner.

Pearl nodded. "I remember."

"Your turn, Pearl," said Ms. Star.

"I made a trash-eating robot," said Pearl. She looked at Wagner. He was slumped down in his seat.

"Wagner and I made it together," said Pearl.

Wagner sat right up again.

Pearl pulled the robot's string. She pulled too hard. The robot's head fell off.

"Uh-oh," said Wagner.

"I guess you two friends have more work to do," said Ms. Star.

"I guess so," said Pearl. "But I don't mind, because Wagner and I will do all of the work together."

"Uh-oh," said Wagner.

The Science Fair

On Science Fair Day, Pearl and Wagner were still working on their robot. Pearl stretched rubber bands. She held them tight. Wagner stapled them onto the shoe box and the lid.

"That should do it," he said.

The signs in the illustration read:

Look at the ANTS

The ants dig and dig and dig to make tunnels. It's a good life

Plants love music

See the effect of music on planted in the pot marigolds.

Pearl and Wagner hurried to the gym with their robot. They passed a boy with an ant village. They passed a girl playing music for plants. They passed Henry. He had his electric potato hooked up to a tiny Ferris wheel.

Pearl and Wagner set
up their robot.

A judge came over.

"Watch this," said
Pearl. Pearl pulled
the robot's string. Nothing happened.
She pulled harder. The robot's mouth popped
open. The rubber bands flew everywhere.

"Yikes!" said the judge.

"Oh, no!" said Wagner. "There goes our prize!"

"We are not quite ready," Pearl told the judge.

"I will come back in five minutes,"
said the judge.

"I have more rubber bands in my desk," said Pearl. She raced off to get them.

Wagner tapped his foot. He bit his nails. Pearl was taking forever! The judge would be back any second. He had to *do* something.

Wagner looked around. No one was watching him. He pulled the tape off the big box. He opened the back of the robot and slipped inside.

The judge came back. She did not see
Pearl and Wagner. She started to leave.

"Wait!" said the robot.

"Oh, my stars!" said the judge.
"A talking robot!"

Just then Pearl came back.

"You have a nice smile," the robot was telling the judge. "And such pretty eyes."

"Do you think so?" said the judge.

Pearl could not believe her ears.

"Your robot is so smart!" said the judge. "How does it work?"

"Uh . . ." said Pearl. "It is hard to explain."

The judge opened the robot's mouth. She looked inside.

"Hi there!" said Wagner.

"Uh-oh," said Pearl.

The judge gave out the prizes. The girl who played music for plants won first prize. Henry and his electric potato won second prize. The trash-eating robot did not win any prize at all.

"I was only trying to help," Wagner told Pearl.
"I know," said Pearl. "You are a good friend,
Wagner. And you were a pretty good robot too."

Think and Share

Talk About It Do you think this story has a sad or happy ending? Why do you think so?

1. Use the pictures below to retell the story. Then draw a picture of what happens after the story is over.

2. Was the author trying to make you laugh, explain something, or give you information? Explain what makes you think that.

3. What problem do Pearl and Wagner have in the middle of the story? How is it solved at the end?

Look Back and Write Look back at pages 333–335. Why do you think the talking robot didn't win a prize? Use details from the selection.

About the Author and the Illustrator
Kate McMullan

Kate McMullan loves to read. When asked what she wanted to be when she grew up, she always said, "A reader." When she decided to try writing, she moved to New York City.

Read more books by Kate McMullan.

R. W. Alley

R. W. Alley has illustrated many books for children. He says Kate McMullan had been thinking of a dog and a cat as Pearl and Wagner. But when she saw his mouse and his rabbit, she approved.

Robots at home

from *Robots* by Clive Gifford

Robots are coming home. The latest robots are doing useful chores around the house. Home robots need to know their way around a house and be able to communicate with their owners.

Ready for breakfast?

Robots cannot cook your meals yet, but they can carry them to you. Home robots often hold a map of the house in their memory. They also need sensors to know when household objects are in their way.

Beware of the dog.

This robot guard dog patrols the house, checking that everything is safe. If it notices anything wrong, it can take pictures and send them to the owner's cell phone.

Home playmates

PaPeRos wander around the house looking for people to talk to. They can recognize 650 different words and phrases and can speak up to 3,000 words. They can even dance!

Verbs

A word that shows action is a **verb**.

Pearl and Wagner **make** a robot.

The word **make** is a verb. It shows action.
It tells what Pearl and Wagner do.

Write Using Verbs

1. Look on page 323. Write one sentence from this page. Underline the verb.

· ·

2. How did Wagner help Pearl? Use the word *talk* to write one sentence that tells what he did. Underline the verb.

· ·

3. What would you do to make Pearl's robot better? Write some sentences. Underline the verbs.

Let's Talk About
Creative Ideas

Words to Read

picture
school
answer
faraway
parents
wash
company

Read the Words

Dear Grandma,

　　Thank you for your letter and the picture. I took them to school. I had to answer many questions from my friends. I told them that you lived in a faraway place called Korea. I told them that my parents will take me there soon.

　　I must go now and wash my hands. We are having company for dinner.

　　　　Love,
　　　　Juno

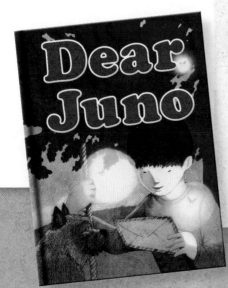

Genre: Realistic Fiction
Realistic fiction has characters, a setting, and a plot that could be real. This next story is about Juno, a boy who finds a creative way to write to his grandmother.

Dear Juno

by Soyung Pak

illustrated by Susan Kathleen Hartung

**Who has written
a letter to Juno?**

Juno watched as the red and white blinking lights soared across the night sky like shooting stars, and waited as they disappeared into faraway places. Juno wondered where they came from. He wondered where they were going. And he wondered if any of the planes came from a little town near Seoul where his grandmother lived, and where she ate persimmons every evening before bed.

355

"Grandma has a new cat," Juno said as he handed the letter to his mother. "And she's growing red and yellow flowers in her garden."

"How do you know she has a new cat?" Juno's father asked.

"She wouldn't send me a picture of a strange cat," said Juno.

"I guess not," said Juno's father.

"How do you know the flower is from her garden?" asked Juno's mother.

"She wouldn't send me a flower from someone else's garden," Juno answered.

"No, she wouldn't," said Juno's mother.

Then Juno's mother read him the letter.

How are you? I have a new cat to keep me company. I named him Juno after you. He can't help me weed, but the rabbits no longer come to eat my flowers.

Grandma

"Just like you read it yourself," Juno's father said.

"I did read it," Juno said.

"Yes, you did," said his mother.

At school, Juno showed his class his grandmother's picture and dried flower. His teacher even pinned the letter to the board. All day long, Juno kept peeking at the flower from his grandmother's garden. He didn't have a garden that grew flowers, but he had a swinging tree.

Juno looked at the letter pinned to the board. Did his grandmother like getting letters too? Yes, Juno thought. She likes getting letters just like I do. So Juno decided to write one.

After school, Juno ran to his backyard. He
picked a leaf from the swinging tree—the
biggest leaf he could find.

Juno found his mother, who was sitting at her
desk. He showed her the leaf. "I'm going to write
a letter," he told her.

"I'm sure it will be a very nice letter," she
answered, and gave him a big yellow envelope.

"Yes it will," Juno said, and then he began
to draw.

First, he drew a picture of his mom and dad standing outside the house. Second, he drew a picture of Sam playing underneath his big swinging tree. Then very carefully, Juno drew a picture of himself standing under an airplane in a starry, nighttime sky. After he was finished, he placed everything in the envelope.

"Here's my letter," Juno announced proudly. "You can read it if you want."

Juno's father looked in the envelope.

He pulled out the leaf. "Only a big swinging
tree could grow a leaf this big," he said.

Juno's mother pulled out one of the drawings.
"What a fine picture," she said. "It takes a good
artist to say so much with a drawing."

Juno's father patted Juno on the head. "It's
just like a real letter," he said.

"It is a real letter," Juno said.

"It certainly is," said his mother. Then they
mailed the envelope and waited.

One day a big envelope came. It was from Juno's grandmother. This time, Juno didn't wait at all. He opened the envelope right away.

Inside, Juno found a box of colored pencils. He knew she wanted another letter.

Next, he pulled out a picture of his grandmother. He noticed she was sitting with a cat and two kittens. He thought for a moment and laughed. Now his grandmother would have to find a new name for her cat—in Korea, Juno was a boy's name, not a girl's.

Then he pulled out a small toy plane.

Juno smiled. His grandmother was coming to visit.

"Maybe she'll bring her cat when she comes to visit," Juno said to Sam as he climbed into bed. "Maybe you two will be friends."

Soon Juno was fast asleep.
And when he dreamed that
night, he dreamed about a
faraway place, a village just
outside Seoul, where his
grandmother, whose gray hair
sat on top of her head like
a powdered doughnut, was
sipping her morning tea.

The cool air feels crisp
against her cheek. Crisp
enough to crackle, he dreams,
like the golden leaves which
cover the persimmon garden.

Think and Share

Talk About It Plan a letter without words to someone. Put three things in the letter, but only one can be a picture. What will you send?

1. Look at the pictures below. They are mixed up. Tell the correct order to retell the story.

2. Can you guess how Juno feels about his grandmother? What makes you think that?

3. What picture did you have in your mind each time Juno spoke of his grandmother? How did visualizing help you?

Look Back and Write Reread page 362. What did a small toy airplane mean to Juno? Use information from the story in your answer.

About the Author and the Illustrator

Soyung Pak

Soyung Pak was born in South Korea. When she was two years old, she moved to New Jersey. When a plane flew overhead, her family waved. They pretended Grandmother was on the plane, coming from Korea.

Read more books by Soyung Pak.

Susan Kathleen Hartung

Susan Hartung has always loved to draw. As a child, she sometimes got in trouble for her pictures. Finally she learned to do her drawings on paper!

SAYING IT WITHOUT WORDS
Signs and Symbols

by Arnulf K. Esterer and Louise A. Esterer

Have you seen signs like these:

- the arrow on a one-way street?
- the EXIT sign over doors in the school auditorium?
- the big letter M over a hamburger shop downtown?

These are a few examples of signs. You have seen many more all around you. A sign tells you exactly what to do or what is there.

Have you seen:

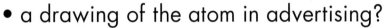

- a happy face on your milk mug?
- the flag of our country waving from a building?
- a drawing of the atom in advertising?

These are a few examples of symbols. They tell about something. Symbols are like pictures of ideas.

Look around. See how many signs and symbols you can find. We use them every day. See how much they help you to know what to do or where to go.

Good signs and symbols tell you something—and fast! They tell you even if you can't read, or even if it's in a foreign language.

One look is all you usually need. One look tells it.

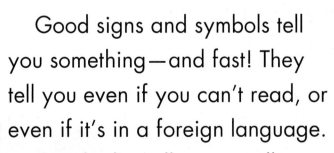

Verbs with Singular and Plural Nouns

Add **-s** to a verb to tell what one person, animal, or thing does.
Do **not** add **-s** to a verb that tells what two or more people, animals, or things do.

Grandma **mails** Juno a letter.

Juno and his mom **mail** a letter to Grandma.

Write Using Verbs with Singular and Plural Nouns

1. Write this sentence using the correct verb.

Juno (pick, picks) a leaf.

. . . .

2. Grandma sent Juno a picture, some crayons, and a toy airplane. Write two sentences that tell Juno what these things mean. Remember to use correct verbs.

. . . .

3. How are Juno's and Grandma's letters alike? How are they different? Write some sentences that tell about the letters. Remember to use verbs correctly.

Let's Talk About
Creative Ideas

Words to Read

believe
caught
finally
been
whatever
today
tomorrow

Read the Words

"I do believe you are stuck," said the spider to the fly who was caught in his web.

"Finally," said the clever fly to the spider. "I've been waiting for you."

"Whatever do you mean?" the spider asked, surprised.

"You invited me over today," the fly said. "Why would you set a trap for your friend?"

The confused spider helped free the fly.

As the fly flew off, he called, "Better clever today than lunch tomorrow!"

Genre: Folk Tale
A folk tale is a story that has been handed down over many years. Now, you will read about how Anansi the Spider is tricked by Turtle.

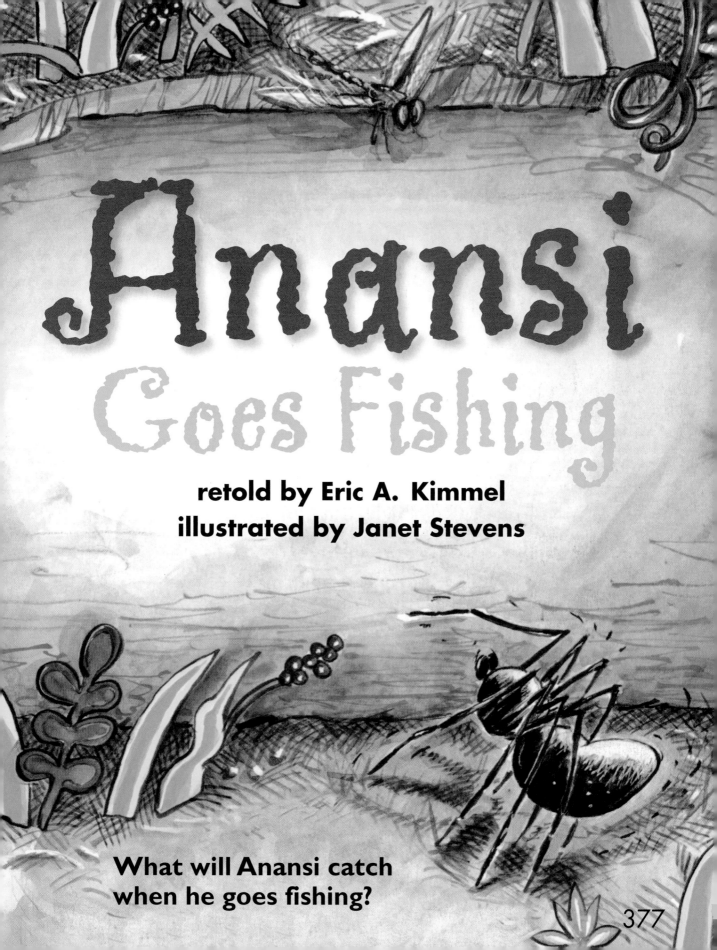

Anansi
Goes Fishing

retold by Eric A. Kimmel
illustrated by Janet Stevens

**What will Anansi catch
when he goes fishing?**

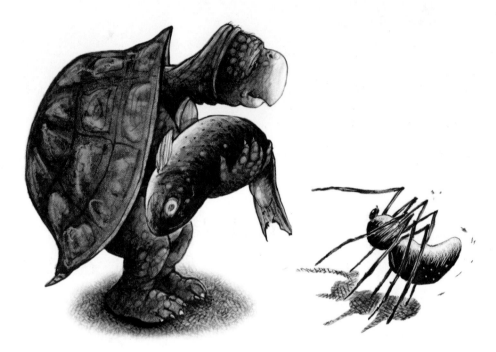

One fine afternoon Anansi the Spider was walking by the river when he saw his friend Turtle coming toward him carrying a large fish. Anansi loved to eat fish, though he was much too lazy to catch them himself.

"Where did you get that fish?" he asked Turtle.

"I caught it today when I went fishing," Turtle replied.

"I want to learn to catch fish too," Anansi said. "Will you teach me?"

"Certainly!" said Turtle. "Meet me by the river tomorrow. We will go fishing together. Two can do twice the work of one."

But Anansi did not intend to do any work at all. "Turtle is slow and stupid," he said to himself. "I will trick him into doing all the work. Then I will take the fish for myself." But Turtle was not as stupid as Anansi thought.

Early the next morning, Turtle arrived. "Are you ready to get started, Anansi?" he asked.

"Yes!" Anansi said. "I have been waiting a long time. I want to learn to catch fish as well as you do."

"First we make a net," said Turtle. "Netmaking is hard work. When I do it myself, I work and get tired. But since there are two of us, we can share the task. One of us can work while the other gets tired."

"I don't want to get tired," Anansi said. "I'll make the net. You can get tired."

"All right," said Turtle. He showed Anansi how to weave a net. Then he lay down on the riverbank.

"This is hard work," Anansi said.

"I know," said Turtle, yawning. "I'm getting very tired."

Anansi worked all day weaving the net. The harder he worked, the more tired Turtle grew. Turtle yawned and stretched, and finally he went to sleep. After many hours the net was done.

"Wake up, Turtle," Anansi said. "The net is finished."

Turtle rubbed his eyes. "This net is strong and light. You are a fine netmaker, Anansi. I know you worked hard because I am very tired. I am so tired, I have to go home and sleep. Meet me here tomorrow. We will catch fish then."

The next morning Turtle met Anansi by the river again.

"Today we are going to set the net in the river," Turtle said. "That is hard work. Yesterday you worked while I got tired, so today I'll work while you get tired."

"No, no!" said Anansi. "I would rather work than get tired."

"All right," said Turtle. So while Anansi worked hard all day setting the net in the river, Turtle lay on the riverbank, getting so tired he finally fell asleep.

"Wake up, Turtle," Anansi said, hours later. "The net is set. I'm ready to start catching fish."

Turtle yawned. "I'm too tired to do any more today, Anansi. Meet me here tomorrow morning. We'll catch fish then."

Turtle met Anansi on the riverbank the next morning.

"I can hardly wait to catch fish," Anansi said.

"That's good," Turtle replied. "Catching fish is hard work. You worked hard these past two days, Anansi. I think I should work today and let you get tired."

"Oh, no!" said Anansi. "I want to catch fish. I don't want to get tired."

"All right," said Turtle. "Whatever you wish."

Anansi worked hard all day pulling the net out of the river while Turtle lay back, getting very, very tired.

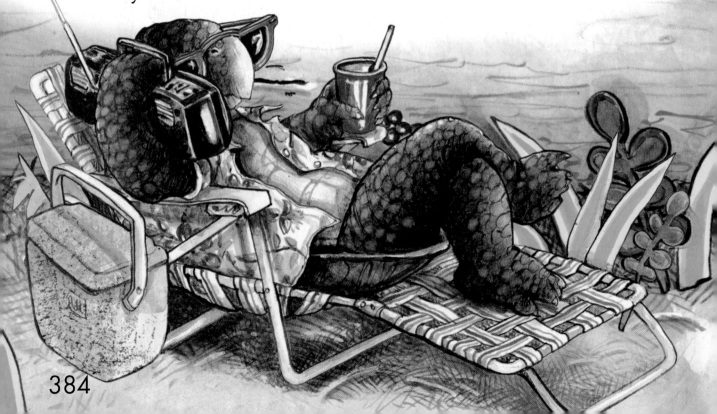

How pleased Anansi was to find a large fish caught in the net!

"What do we do now?" he asked Turtle.

Turtle yawned. "Now we cook the fish. Cooking is hard work. I think I should cook while you get tired."

"No!" cried Anansi. He did not want to share any bit of the fish. "I will cook. You get tired."

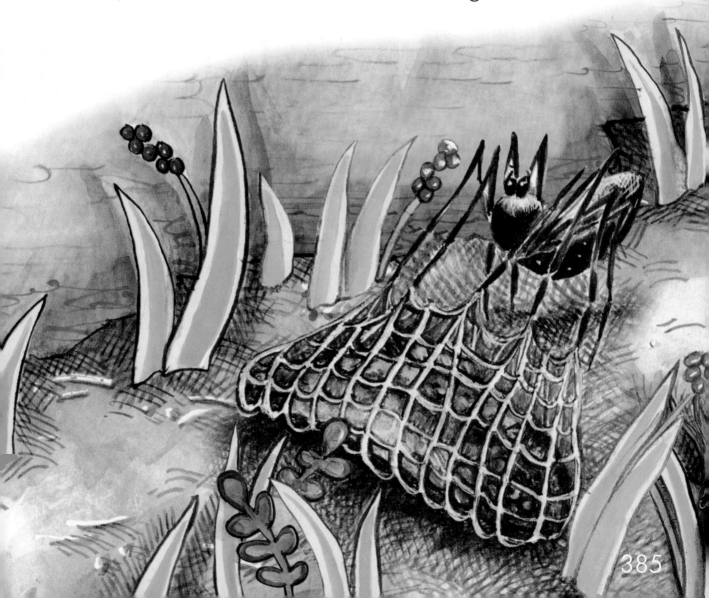

   While Turtle watched, Anansi built a fire and
cooked the fish from head to tail.

   "That fish smells delicious," Turtle said. "You
are a good cook, Anansi. And you worked hard.
I know, because I am very, very tired. Now it is
time to eat the fish. When I eat by myself, I eat
and get full. Since there are two of us, we should
share the task. One of us should eat while the
other gets full. Which do you want to do?"

   "I want to get full!" Anansi said, thinking only
of his stomach.

   "Then I will eat." Turtle began to eat while
Anansi lay back and waited for his stomach to
get full.

"Are you full yet?" Turtle asked Anansi.
"Not yet. Keep eating."

Turtle ate some more. "Are you full yet?"
"No. Keep eating."

Turtle ate some more. "Are you full yet?"
"Not at all," Anansi said. "I'm as empty
as when you started."

"That's too bad," Turtle told him. "Because I'm full, and all the fish is gone."

"What?" Anansi cried. It was true. Turtle had eaten the whole fish. "You cheated me!" Anansi yelled when he realized what had happened.

"I did not!" Turtle replied.

"You did! You made me do all the work, then you ate the fish yourself. You won't get away with this. I am going to the Justice Tree."

Anansi ran to the Justice Tree. Warthog sat beneath its branches. Warthog was a fair and honest judge. All the animals brought their quarrels to him.

"What do you want, Anansi?" Warthog asked.

"I want justice," Anansi said. "Turtle cheated me. We went fishing together. He tricked me into doing all the work, then he ate the fish himself. Turtle deserves to be punished."

Warthog knew how lazy Anansi was. He couldn't imagine him working hard at anything. "Did you really do all the work?" he asked.

"Yes," Anansi replied.

"What did you do?"

"I wove the net.

I set it in the river.

I caught the fish,

and I cooked it."

"That is a lot of work. You must have gotten very tired."

"No," said Anansi. "I didn't get tired at all. Turtle got tired, not me."

Warthog frowned. "Turtle got tired? What did he do?"

"Nothing!"

"If he did nothing, why did he get tired? Anansi, I don't believe you. No one gets tired by doing nothing. If Turtle got tired, then he must have done all the work. You are not telling the truth. Go home now and stop making trouble."

393

Warthog had spoken. There was nothing more to be said. Anansi went home in disgrace, and it was a long time before he spoke to Turtle again.

But some good came out of it. Anansi learned how to weave nets and how to use them to catch food. He taught his friends how to do it, and they taught their friends. Soon spiders all over the world were weaving. To this day, wherever you find spiders, you will find their nets.

They are called "spider webs."

Think and Share

Talk About It What three rules would you give Anansi and Turtle to follow if they go fishing again?

1. The pictures below show what happens in the middle of the story. On another piece of paper draw what happens at the beginning and at the end of the story.

2. What happens to make Anansi so angry? Look back at page 389. Read that part.

3. A lot happens in this story. What did you do to make sure you didn't miss anything?

Look Back and Write Reread pages 390–393. Why didn't Justice Warthog believe Anansi's story? Use information from the story to support your answer.

Meet the Author
Eric Kimmel

Read more books by Eric Kimmel about Anansi.

ANANSI and the MAGIC STICK
by Eric A. Kimmel
illustrated by Janet Stevens

Anansi and the Moss-Covered Rock
retold by Eric A. Kimmel
illustrated by Janet Stevens

Eric Kimmel first heard stories about Anansi as a child in New York City. He also heard Anansi stories from neighbors when he lived in the Virgin Islands. The stories come from Africa and are very old. "I enjoyed telling the stories so much that I tried my hand at writing them."

Mr. Kimmel says, "I like spiders. I never kill one. If I find a spider in the house, I catch it and take it outside. Spiders do us a lot of good, catching flies and other insect pests."

Meet the Illustrator

Janet Stevens

Before Janet Stevens drew Anansi, she read books about spiders. She thought about how to show Anansi's personality. "I mainly did it through his movement and gestures. He doesn't have a lot of face." She didn't want Anansi to look cute. "I like Anansi," she says. "He likes to get out of working."

Read two more books by Janet Stevens.

Ms. Stevens has written and illustrated many children's books. She enjoys drawing wrinkles. "My favorite characters are rhinos, iguanas— anything with lots of wrinkles."

Do spiders stick to their own webs?

by Amy Goldman Koss

The spider weaves a sticky web
To capture bugs to eat.
What keeps the spider's sticky web
From sticking to her feet?

Spiderwebs are very tricky
Because not all the strands are sticky.
Unlike the passing hapless fly,
The spider knows which strands are dry.

But if by accident she stands
On any of the sticky strands,
She still would not get stuck, you see—
Her oily body slides off free.

Verbs for Present, Past, and Future

Use different forms of a verb to tell about present, past, and future action.

Today Anansi **waits** for Turtle.

The verb **waits** tells about now.

Yesterday Anansi **waited** for Turtle.

The verb **waited** tells about the past. It ends with **-ed**.

Tomorrow Anansi **will wait** for Turtle.

The verb **will wait** tells about the future. It begins with **will**.

Write Using Verbs for Present, Past, and Future

1. Write each of these verbs so that they tell about the past and future.

tricks   starts   shows

. . . .

2. This sentence tells about the past.

Anansi worked hard.

Write the sentence again, once to show present action and once to show future action. Underline the verb in each sentence.

. . . .

3. Write some sentences comparing what Anansi did with what Turtle did. Use verbs that tell about present action. Underline the verbs.

Let's Talk About
Creative Ideas

Words to Read

daughters

youngest

their

buy

many

alone

half

Read the Words

Rosa and Blanca are the daughters of a very loving mother. Rosa is the youngest. Their mother can't buy them many things, but she gives them lots of love. The two girls know that they will never be alone. They say that they will be happy if they can find in themselves half as much love as their mother gives.

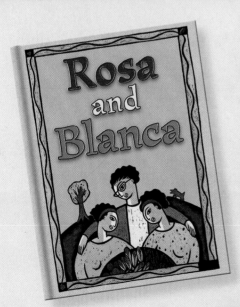

Genre: Realistic Fiction
Realistic fiction is a made-up story that could really happen. Next you will read about Rosa and Blanca, two sisters with a clever idea.

Rosa and Blanca

by Joe Hayes

illustrated by José Ortega

Who are Rosa and Blanca, and what is their creative idea?

Once there were two sisters named Rosa and Blanca. They loved each other very much. If their mother sent Rosa to the store to buy flour for tortillas, Blanca would go with her. If their mother told Blanca to sweep the sidewalk in front of their house, Rosa would help her.

Their mother would always say, "My daughters are so good to one another. They make me very happy. I think I am the luckiest mother in the town. No. I am the luckiest mother in the country. No. I am the luckiest mother in the whole world!"

When Rosa and Blanca grew up, Rosa got married. She and her husband had three children. Blanca didn't get married. She lived alone.

One year Rosa planted a garden. Blanca planted a garden too. They planted corn and tomatoes and good hot *chiles*.

When the tomatoes were round and ripe, Rosa helped Blanca pick the tomatoes in her garden. Blanca helped Rosa pick the tomatoes in her garden.

That night Rosa thought, "My poor sister Blanca lives all alone. She has no one to help her make a living. I have a husband and helpful children. I will give her half of my tomatoes to sell in the market."

Rosa filled a basket with tomatoes. She started toward Blanca's house.

That very same night Blanca thought, "My poor sister Rosa has a husband and three children. There are five to feed in her house. I only have myself. I will give her half of my tomatoes to sell in the market."

Blanca filled a basket with tomatoes. She started toward Rosa's house. The night was dark. The two sisters did not see each other when they passed.

Rosa added her tomatoes to the pile in Blanca's kitchen. Blanca added her tomatoes to the pile in Rosa's kitchen.

The next day, Rosa looked at her pile of tomatoes. "*¡Vaya!*" she said. "How can I have so many tomatoes? Did my tomatoes have babies during the night?"

The next day Blanca looked at her pile of tomatoes. "¡Vaya!" she said. "How can I have so many tomatoes? Did my tomatoes have babies during the night?"

When the corn was ripe, Rosa helped Blanca pick her corn. Blanca helped Rosa pick her corn.

That night Rosa thought, "I will give half of my corn to Blanca to sell in the market."

That night Blanca thought, "I will give half of my corn to Rosa to sell in the market."

Each sister filled a basket with corn. Rosa went to Blanca's house. Blanca went to Rosa's house. The night was dark. They did not see each other when they passed.

Rosa added her corn to the corn in Blanca's house. Blanca added her corn to the corn in Rosa's house.

The next day Rosa said, "¡Vaya! How can I have so much corn? Did each ear invite a friend to spend the night?"

The next day Blanca said, "¡Vaya! How can I have so much corn? Did each ear invite a friend to spend the night?"

When the chiles were red and hot, Rosa helped Blanca pick her chiles. Blanca helped Rosa pick her chiles.

That night Rosa thought, "I will give Blanca half of my chiles to sell in the market."

That night Blanca thought, "I will give Rosa half of my chiles to sell in the market."

Each sister filled a basket with chiles.

Just then Rosa's youngest child started to cry. Rosa went to the child's room. She picked him up and rocked him.

Blanca was on her way to Rosa's house.

When Rosa's child went to sleep, Rosa picked up her basket of chiles. She started out the door. Blanca was coming in the door.

They both said, "¡Vaya!"

Rosa said, "Blanca, what are you doing? Why do you have that basket of chiles?"

Blanca said, "Rosa, what are you doing? Why do you have that basket of chiles?"

Rosa said, "I was going to give half of my chiles to you."

Blanca said, "But I was going to give half of my chiles to you!" Both sisters laughed.

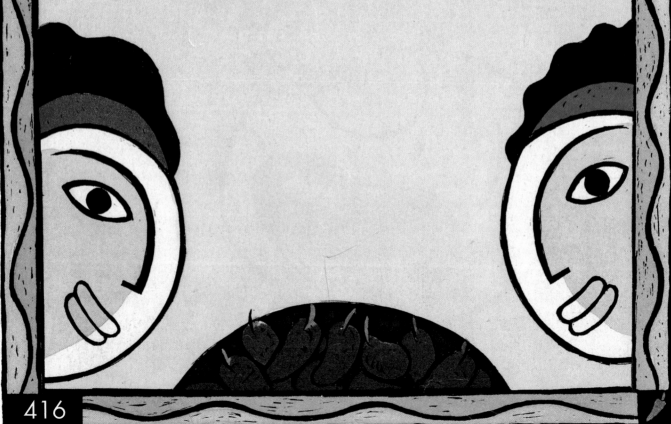

Rosa said, "So that is why I still had so many tomatoes!"

Blanca said, "So that is why I still had so much corn!" The sisters hugged each other.

The next day Rosa and Blanca went to their mother's house. They told their mother what they had done.

Their old mother smiled and hugged her daughters. She said, "My daughters are so good to one another. They make me very happy. I think I am the luckiest mother in the town. No. I am the luckiest mother in the country. No. I am the luckiest mother in the whole world!"

Think and Share

Talk About It Rosa and Blanca had a clever idea that went wrong. Now they are planting again. What will you tell them so that they will not have another mix-up?

1. Use the pictures below to retell the story.

2. What was the big idea of this story? What do you think the characters learned?

3. What did you predict the sisters would do with their vegetables? Were you right? Did you change any predictions as you read?

Look Back and Write Look back in the story. Name three things that Rosa and Blanca planted.

About the Author
Joe Hayes

Joe Hayes grew up listening to stories told by his father. He liked hearing stories so much that he decided he wanted to tell them too. Mr. Hayes began by telling stories to his own children. He soon realized that he liked telling stories to as many children as he could!

Mr. Hayes travels to many different places to share with children the stories he has learned. He has also published 20 books, many in English and Spanish.

Read more books by Joe Hayes.

The Crow and the Pitcher

a fable by Aesop retold by Eric Blair
illustrated by Laura Ovresat

There was once a thirsty crow. She had flown a long way looking for water.

The thirsty crow saw a pitcher of water and flew down to drink.

The pitcher had only a little water left at the bottom.

The crow put her beak into the pitcher. The water was so low she couldn't reach it.

*But I must have water to drink.
I can't fly any farther,* thought
the crow.

I know. I'll tip the pitcher over,
she thought.

The thirsty crow beat the pitcher
with her wings, but she wasn't
strong enough to tip it.

*Maybe I can break the pitcher. Then
the water will flow,* thought the crow.

She backed away to get a flying start. With all her might, the thirsty crow flew at the pitcher. She struck it with her pointed beak and claws, but the tired crow wasn't strong enough to break the pitcher.

Just as she was about to give up, the crow had another idea. She dropped a pebble into the pitcher. The water rose a little.

She dropped another and
another. With each pebble, the
water level rose more.

Soon the water reached the
brim. The crow drank until she
was no longer thirsty.

The crow was pleased with
herself. By refusing to give
up, she had solved her
difficult problem.

More About Verbs

. . . .

Use the correct verb in a sentence to show that something is happening now, in the past, or in the future.

. . . .

Today Rosa and Blanca **plant** a garden. (now)

Yesterday they **planted** corn. (past)

Tomorrow they **will plant** tomatoes. (future)

Write Using More Verbs

1. This sentence tells about the present.

Rosa helps Blanca.

Write the sentence again to show the past. Then write the sentence to show the future. Underline the verb in each sentence.

• •

2. In what ways can Rosa and Blanca help their mother? Write two sentences using verbs to tell about the future. Tell what the girls will do. Underline the verbs.

• •

3. Rosa and Blanca are very much alike. They are also different. Write some sentences that compare the two girls. Use verbs that tell about present action. Underline the verb in each sentence.

Let's Talk About
Creative Ideas

Words to Read

neighbor
hours
money
clothes
taught
only
question

Read the Words

Our neighbor spends many hours in his beautiful garden. He doesn't make a lot of money, and he wears torn clothes. However, he loves his plants and flowers. He taught himself a lot of what he knows. I have only one question for him. Can he teach me too?

A Weed Is a Flower

Genre: Biography
A biography tells about a real person's life. It is written by another person. Next you will read the biography of George Washington Carver, a creative scientist.

430

A Weed Is a Flower

The Life of George Washington Carver
by Aliki

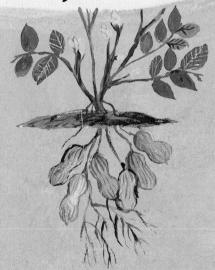

Who was George Washington Carver?

George Washington Carver was born in Missouri in 1860—more than a hundred years ago. It was a terrible time. Mean men rode silently in the night, kidnapping slaves from their owners and harming those who tried to stop them.

One night, a band of these men rode up to the farm of Moses Carver, who owned George and his mother, Mary. Everyone ran in fear. But before Mary could hide her baby, the men came and snatched them both, and rode away into the night.

Moses Carver sent a man to look for them.
Mary was never found. But in a few days, the man
returned with a small bundle wrapped in his coat
and tied to the back of his saddle. It was the
baby, George.

Moses and his wife, Susan, cared for Mary's
children. George remained small and weak. But
as he grew, they saw he was an unusual child. He
wanted to know about everything around him. He
asked about the rain, the flowers, and the insects.
He asked questions the Carvers couldn't answer.

When he was very young, George kept a garden where he spent hours each day caring for his plants. If they weren't growing well, he found out why. Soon they were healthy and blooming. In winter he covered his plants to protect them. In spring he planted new seeds. George looked after each plant as though it was the only one in his garden.

Neighbors began to ask George's advice about their plants, and soon he was known as the Plant Doctor.

As time went on, George wondered about more and more things. He wanted to learn and yearned to go to school.

In the meantime, the slaves had been freed, but schools nearby were not open to blacks. So when he was ten, George left his brother, his garden, and the Carver farm and went off to find the answers to his questions.

Wherever George Washington Carver found schools, he stayed. He worked for people to earn his keep. He scrubbed their floors, washed their clothes, and baked their bread. Whatever George did, he did well. Even the smallest chore was important to him.

Some people took George in as their son. First he stayed with Mariah and Andy Watkins, who were like parents to him. Then he moved to Kansas and lived with "Aunt" Lucy and "Uncle" Seymour. They, too, loved this quiet boy who was so willing to help.

437

George worked hard for many years, always trying to save enough money for college. Other boys, who had parents to help them, were able to enter college much sooner than George. He was thirty before he had saved enough. Still, it was not that simple. Not all colleges would admit blacks, even if they had the money to pay.

George was not discouraged. He moved to Iowa and found a college which was glad to have a black student.

At college, George continued to work. He opened a laundry where he washed his schoolmates' clothes.

And, he continued to learn. His teachers and friends soon realized that this earnest young man was bursting with talents. He played the piano, he sang beautifully, and he was an outstanding painter. In fact, for a time he thought of becoming an artist.

440

But the more George thought of what he wanted to do, the more he wanted to help his people. And he remembered that his neighbors used to call him the Plant Doctor.

He had never forgotten his love for plants. In all the years he had wandered, he always had something growing in his room.

So, George Washington Carver chose to study agriculture. He learned about plants, flowers, and soil. He learned the names of the weeds. Even they were important to him. He often said: a weed is a flower growing in the wrong place.

He still asked questions. If no person or book could answer them, he found the answers himself. He experimented with his own plants, and found secrets no one else knew.

441

When George finished college, he began to teach. He was asked to go to Alabama, where a college for blacks needed his talent. It was there, at Tuskegee Institute, that George Washington Carver made his life.

In Alabama, Professor Carver taught his students and the poor black farmers, who earned their livelihood from the soil. He taught them how to make their crops grow better.

443

Most of the farmers raised cotton. But sometimes the crops were destroyed by rain or insects, and the farmers couldn't earn enough to eat.

Professor Carver told them to plant other things as well. Sweet potatoes and peanuts were good crops. They were easy to grow. He said that raising only cotton harmed the soil. It was better if different crops were planted each year.

The farmers did not want to listen. They were afraid to plant peanuts and sweet potatoes. They were sure that no one would buy them.

But Professor Carver had experimented in his laboratory. He had found that many things could be made from the sweet potato. He made soap, coffee, and starch. He made more than a hundred things from the sweet potato.

And even though people in those days called peanuts "monkey food," Professor Carver said they were good for people, too. Besides, he found that still more things could be made from the peanut. Paper, ink, shaving cream, sauces, linoleum, shampoo, and even milk! In fact, he made three hundred different products from the peanut.

Once, when important guests were expected at Tuskegee, Dr. Carver chose the menu. The guests sat around the table and enjoyed a meal of soup, creamed mock chicken, bread, salad, coffee, candy, cake, and ice cream. Imagine their surprise when they learned that the meal was made entirely from peanuts!

Slowly, the farmers listened to George Washington Carver. They planted peanuts and sweet potatoes. Before they knew it these became two of the most important crops in Alabama.

Soon the whole country knew about Dr. Carver and the great things he was doing. He was honored by Presidents and other important people. Every day, his mailbox bulged with letters from farmers and scientists who wanted his advice. He was offered great sums of money, which he turned down. Money was not important to him. He did not even bother to cash many of the checks he received.

Throughout his life, George Washington Carver asked nothing of others. He sought only to help. He lived alone and tended to his own needs. He washed his clothes and patched them, too. He used the soap he made and ate the food he grew.

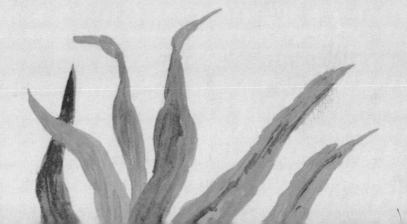

Dr. Carver was asked to speak in many parts of the world, but he did not leave Tuskegee often. He had things to do. He continued to paint. He worked in his greenhouse and in his laboratory, where he discovered many things. He discovered that dyes could be made from plants, and colors from the Alabama clay. Even when he was over eighty and close to death, Dr. Carver kept working. Night after night, while the rest of the town lay asleep, a light still shone in his window.

The baby born with no hope for the future grew into one of the great scientists of his country. George Washington Carver, with his goodness and devotion, helped not only his own people, but all peoples of the world.

Think and Share

Talk About It If you could visit Dr. Carver, would you visit when he was a boy, a young man, or a famous professor? Tell about your visit.

1. Use the pictures below to summarize what you learned.

2. What caused the farmers to start planting peanuts and sweet potatoes?

3. How did you look for the answer to question 2? Did you read every word? Did you skim and scan? Which way is best? Why?

Look Back and Write Look back at page 445. Why did Dr. Carver tell farmers to plant sweet potatoes and peanuts?

About the Author and Illustrator
Aliki

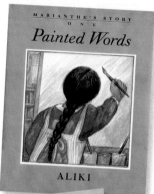

When Aliki writes a book, she often uses cartoons and draws funny characters talking in the margins. Her books are fun, but she does lots of research. "I spend many hours at my desk," she says. "Some books take three years to finish. That's why I call what I do hard fun."

Aliki grew up in Philadelphia, but her parents are from Greece. She speaks Greek as well as English. She prefers to use only her first name on her books.

Read two more books by Aliki.

What's Made from Corn?

If you are writing a report, you can use the Internet to help find information. Maria wants to give a report on how corn is used every day. She does an Internet search using a search engine. First, Maria brainstorms a list of keywords about her topic. These can be single words or groups of words that she will type into the search window of a search engine. Maria came up with these keywords:

> **Corn**
>
> **Uses of corn**
>
> **How we use corn**

She can type any of these into a search engine window and then click the Search button. After a few seconds, she gets a list of Web sites.

Take It to the NET
ONLINE
more activities sfsuccessnet.com

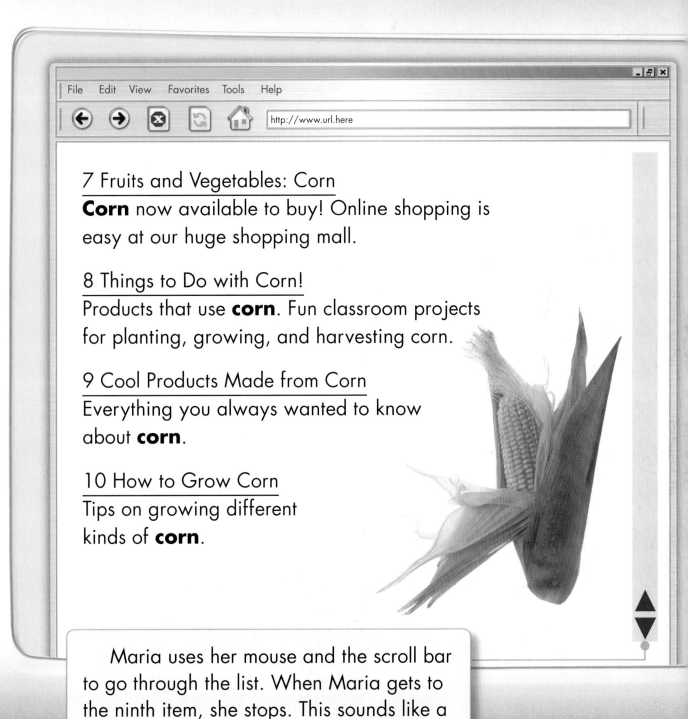

7 Fruits and Vegetables: Corn
Corn now available to buy! Online shopping is easy at our huge shopping mall.

8 Things to Do with Corn!
Products that use **corn**. Fun classroom projects for planting, growing, and harvesting corn.

9 Cool Products Made from Corn
Everything you always wanted to know about **corn**.

10 How to Grow Corn
Tips on growing different kinds of **corn**.

Maria uses her mouse and the scroll bar to go through the list. When Maria gets to the ninth item, she stops. This sounds like a helpful Web site.

Maria clicks on the link <u>Cool Products Made from</u> <u>Corn</u>. This link has many pictures and descriptions. The next thing Maria sees on her computer screen is:

File   Edit   View   Favorites   Tools   Help

http://www.url.here

Cool Products Made from Corn

- Corn can be used to make knives, forks, and spoons. Corn can be used to make plates, diapers, milk jugs, razors, and golf tees. All these things dissolve when put into the garbage. This helps the environment.

- Corn can be made into "packing peanuts." Packing peanuts are used to protect objects packed in boxes. These peanuts dissolve in water.

Cool Products Made from Corn

- Corn is also used to make soap for washing your clothes. This soap cleans better.

- Corn oil can be used to make paints and dyes that do not pollute our world.

- Corn can be used to make the film used in your camera.

Maria takes notes and then looks up more Web sites. After finding out more facts, she can report on the many different ways corn is used.

457

Am, Is, Are, Was, and Were

The verbs **am, is, are, was,** and **were** do not show action. They show what someone or something is or was. These are forms of the verb *to be*.

Use **am, is,** and **was** to tell about one person, place, or thing.
Use **are** and **were** to tell about more than one person, place, or thing.

I **am** a farmer.
George **is** the Plant Doctor.
The Carvers **are** farmers.

The verbs **am, is,** and **are** tell about now.

George **was** a weak child.
Mariah and Andy **were** parents to him.

The verbs **was** and **were** tell about the past.

Write Using Am, Is, Are, Was, and Were

1. Look on page 431. Find a sentence that uses *am*, *is*, *are*, *was*, or *were.* Write it. Underline the verb.

- -

2. What question would you like to ask George Washington Carver? Use *am*, *is*, *are*, *was*, or *were* in your question. Underline the verb.

- -

3. Write some sentences to compare and contrast George's life as a little boy and as a man. Use *am*, *is*, *are*, *was*, and *were* in your sentences.

Wrap-Up

Write a Letter

Juno and his grandma sent letters to each other. Choose a character from one of the stories in this unit. Write a letter to him or her. What would you write? Will you give Wagner advice? Will you tell Anansi a joke? Be creative. Use words in your letter, but also include a picture or other object that will mean something to your character.

Dear Anansi,

What does it mean to be creative?

Creative Characters

connect to SOCIAL STUDIES

Each story you read in this unit had at least one character who was creative. With a group, talk about each story. Tell how the characters acted in creative ways. Tell how an idea from each story could help you do something in a creative way. Make a chart of your ideas.

Story	Character	What they did	My idea

Step by Step

connect to SCIENCE

When Pearl made a robot for her science project, she explained what she was doing step by step. Think of a creative project you might do. Write a set of step-by-step directions that someone else could follow.

How to make a chocolate chip pizza

What you need:
pizza dough
chocolate chips
strawberries
whipped cream

What you do:
First you spread the dough on the pan.

Strategies

100% *GREAT JOB!*

How to Answer Questions

You will answer many kinds of questions. Here are three kinds.

A Question with ⟶
Three Answers

> **Tip:** Only one answer is right. You must find the right answer.

1 What did Jack sell?

- ◯ a handful of beans
- ◑ his cow
- ◯ a beanstalk

Complete the ⟶
Sentence

> **Tip:** Only one answer is right. Make sure your answer makes sense in the sentence.

2 At the top of the beanstalk lived a

- ◑ giant.
- ◯ king.
- ◯ troll.

Write the Answer ⟶

> **Tip:** Use complete sentences when you write your answers. Be clear.

3 What happened to the giant at the end of the story?

He fell to the ground.

Try It!

Use what you learned to answer this question.

4 The test questions on these pages are about

○ "The Three Bears."

○ "Cinderella."

○ "Jack and the Beanstalk."

Questions

EXCELLENT!

100%

Understand the Question

You must understand a test question before you can answer it. Follow these steps.

- **Look for key words.** Key words tell you what the question is asking.

- **Ask yourself:** "What do I need to find out?"

A story about "The Three Bears" may have this question.

1 Whose soup did Goldilocks eat up?

◯ Papa Bear's soup

◯ Mama Bear's soup

◯ Baby Bear's soup

The key words are highlighted. You need to find out whose soup Goldilocks ate up. You know she liked Baby Bear's soup. The last answer must be the correct one.

464

Try It!

What do you need to find out in order to answer these questions about "The Three Bears"?

1 What happened to Baby Bear's chair?

◯ It broke.

◯ It got slippery.

◯ It stayed the same.

2 Who had the biggest bed?

◯ Papa Bear

◯ Mama Bear

◯ Baby Bear

100%

SUPER!

In the Book

Sometimes the answers to test questions are **in the book.** You can find these answers right in the text.

Right There

- The answer is RIGHT THERE in one spot in the text.
- The answer is usually easy to find.
- You can put your finger on the answer.

Think and Search

- The answer IS in the text, but NOT in one spot.
- You need to SEARCH for the answer in different parts of the text.
- You need to THINK about how to put the information together.

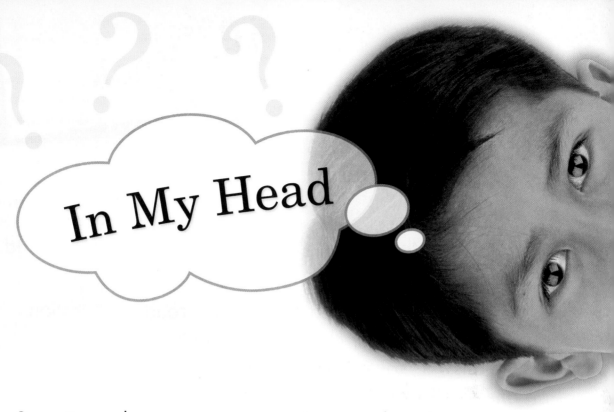

In My Head

Sometimes the answers to questions are **in your head.** The answers are NOT right there in the text.

Author and Me

- The answer is NOT written in the text.

- The AUTHOR gives you clues about the answer.

- You also must use what YOU already know.

- You put all this together to FIGURE OUT the best answer.

On My Own

- The answer is NOT in the text at all.

- You must THINK about what YOU already know.

- You need to use your prior knowledge to figure out the answer.

Right There

Where can you find the answer to a test question? Sometimes the answer is RIGHT THERE in what you read. You can put your finger on the answer.

Read the paragraph below. Then read the question and all the answer choices. The highlighted words are the answer. You can see that the answer is in just one sentence.

The answer is RIGHT THERE.

In the 1840s many settlers **moved west.** The trip was long and hard. They had to cross the Rocky Mountains before they could complete their trip in California or Oregon.

1 When did the settlers **move west**?

◯ in 1800

◉ in the 1840s

◯ in California

The key words are in dark letters. Look at the key words in the question. Look for the same key words in the text. Find the answer near the key words.

Try It!

Now read this paragraph. Then read the question and all the answer choices. Look for a key word in the question. Find the key word in the paragraph. Can you find the answer RIGHT THERE in the text too? Point to it. Then choose the correct answer.

Thousands of settlers traveled the Oregon Trail to get to the West. Setting out from Independence, Missouri, they followed the trail for more than 2,000 miles. Imagine how glad they were when they reached Oregon City, the end of the trail!

1 Where did the Oregon Trail end?

- ○ at Independence, Missouri
- ○ at Oregon City
- ○ in California

Look for the key word *end* in the paragraph.

2 How long was the Oregon Trail?

- ○ more than 2,000 meters
- ○ more than 2,000 feet
- ○ more than 2,000 miles

Remember that the answers to some test questions are RIGHT THERE in the text. Test questions that start with these words often have the answers right there:
who   what   where   when

I Can Find the Answer

In the Book

Think and Search

Sometimes you can't find the answer to a question in just one sentence. You may need to SEARCH in two or more sentences. Then you need to THINK about how to put the information together to get the answer.

Read the paragraph below. Then read the question and answer choices. Look at the two sentences that have highlights. Both sentences will give you information about the answer.

SEARCH for the information in different sentences. THINK about what you know from them.

> **Rat-a-tat-tat!** It sounded like someone was hammering outside. *Who could it be*, thought Pete? He was surprised when he looked out the window. A busy woodpecker was pecking at the water pipe.

key word

1 Who made the **rat-a-tat-tat** sound?

- ○ Pete
- ○ a house builder
- ● a woodpecker

The key word in the question is **rat-a-tat-tat**. Now go back to the paragraph. Is the answer near that key word? That sentence does not have *all* of the answer. The rest of the answer is in the last sentence.

470

Try It!

Now answer the questions that go with the paragraph below. Remember that sometimes you need to SEARCH for the answer in more than one place. Then you must THINK about what you already know.

In the spring Tim planted a vegetable garden with his sister Kate. They planted carrots, corn, onions, and beans. In August all their vegetables were grown. Tim and Kate decided to open a vegetable stand. They sold out of everything but the onions.

1 When did Tim and Kate open their vegetable stand?

○ in the spring

○ in August

○ in the fall

Look for key words in the question. Search for them in the paragraph.

2 What did they sell out of?

○ carrots, corn, onions, and beans

○ carrots, corn, and beans

○ onions

Remember that the answer to some questions may be in more than one spot.

I Can Find the Answer

In My Head

 Author and Me

The answers to some questions are NOT right there in the text. You need to read and FIGURE IT OUT! Follow these steps to answer Author and Me questions.

- Use information that the AUTHOR gives you.
- Use what YOU already know.
- Put the two together to get the answer.

Read the paragraph below about Mike and Troy. Then read the question and all the answer choices.

Mike and Troy have lots of fun together. They like to play video games and work puzzles. They like to read books. But most of all, they like to play ball sports.

> The AUTHOR uses different details. One detail is "ball sports." What YOU know about ball sports will help you answer the question.

1 Which of these things would Mike and Troy like to do most?

- play soccer
- go swimming
- read a mystery

The author doesn't use details like *soccer* or *mysteries*. The author does say that Mike and Troy like to play ball sports the most. You know that soccer is a ball sport. The first answer must be the correct one.

Try It!

Now read the paragraph and questions below. You need to read the text to get important information from the AUTHOR. Then remember to use what YOU know to choose the best answer.

On his birthday Mike woke up feeling very excited. Then he looked out the window. Rain was pouring down. "Oh no," Mike groaned. "This will ruin my birthday party. Now we can't have a treasure hunt in the backyard." Suddenly, Mike smiled. Treasure hunts inside big, dark basements could be fun too.

1 How does Mike feel about the rain?

○ unhappy

○ happy

○ excited

Remember this about Author and Me: information from the author + information from me = the correct answer.

2 Where will Mike probably have the treasure hunt?

○ in the backyard

○ in the basement

○ in the attic

To predict outcomes, you need to use what the AUTHOR tells you and what YOU already know about how people act.

I Can Find the Answer

In My Head

On My Own

The answer to a question may NOT be in the text. You need to get the answer from your own head. You must THINK about what YOU already know.

Sometimes you need to *write* out the answer for a test or for a question your teacher gives you. Often the test will ask you to write about the *topic* of a text. The topic is the main idea. Then you need to write your ideas clearly. You must give details about what you know.

Read the next paragraph. Then follow the directions. Notice that you do NOT need the text to write your answer.

Maria loved Ham, her little hamster. She liked petting his soft brown fur. She liked watching him stuff his large cheeks with food. Best of all, she liked to watch Ham running on his toy wheel. What a racing star!

The key words are highlighted. They tell the *topic* to write about.

Directions: Write about your favorite pet. It can be a pet you own or one you would like to have. Tell what things you like about the pet.

My favorite pet is a parrot. Parrots are smart. I could teach a parrot new words. A parrot could also ride on my shoulder.

Try It!

Now read the paragraph below. Then follow the directions. Look for key words that tell you what to write about. Remember that sometimes you need to write an answer ON YOUR OWN.

I think we should have our class picnic at the city park. The park has great equipment for climbing and playing. We could feed the ducks on the lake. We could even fly kites on the big hill.

Directions: What if you could take your friends anywhere for a picnic. Tell about where you would go and why you like that place. Use a separate sheet of paper.

 Read the directions carefully. Look for key words that tell you what to write about.

 Remember to give clear details about your OWN ideas.

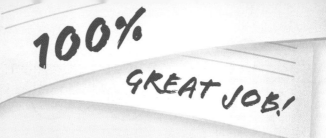
Strategies

	Right There The answer is RIGHT THERE in the text.
	Think and Search The answer IS in the text, but NOT in just one spot.
	Author and Me The answer is NOT in the text. Think about what YOU know and what the AUTHOR tells you.
	On My Own The answer is NOT in the text. Think of the answer ON YOUR OWN.

Try It! Read this selection. Then answer the questions that follow.

Helen Keller

When Helen Keller was two years old, she got very sick. The illness hurt little Helen for the rest of her life. She could never see or hear again.

Helen's life changed when Anne Sullivan came to live with her. Sullivan could "talk" to Helen in a special way. She spelled out words in Helen's hands. It was a language made for deaf people to use.

Helen Keller learned very fast. Soon she was writing letters and stories. When she grew up, she wrote books about her life. She always gave thanks to her first teacher, Anne Sullivan.

Directions: Answer these questions. Write your answers on a separate sheet of paper.

1 When did Helen Keller lose her sight and hearing?

◯ when she was born

◯ when she was two

◯ when Anne Sullivan came

2 What caused Helen to become blind and deaf?

◯ a car accident

◯ a bad fall

◯ a bad illness

3 Who was Helen Keller's first teacher?

◯ Anne Sullivan

◯ her doctor

◯ her publisher

4 Where did Anne Sullivan spell out words for Helen?

◯ on paper

◯ in a book

◯ in her hand

5 What kind of learner was Helen?

◯ quick

◯ slow

◯ sad

6 Which of these books did Helen Keller most likely write?

◯ *Jungle Animals*

◯ *The Story of My Life*

◯ *How to Care for the Sick*

7 Write about a person you admire or look up to. Tell what makes that person special.

Glossary

Aa

agriculture (ag ruh KUL cher) **Agriculture** is farming and growing crops. *NOUN*

amazing (uh MAY zing) Something that is **amazing** is very surprising: The hero made an **amazing** escape. *ADJECTIVE*

astronaut

astronaut (ASS truh nawt) An **astronaut** is a person who has been trained to fly in a spacecraft. While in space, **astronauts** repair space stations and do experiments. *NOUN*

Bb

brave (BRAYV) If you are **brave**, you are not afraid: The **brave** girl pulled her little brother away from the burning leaves. *ADJECTIVE*

buried (BAIR eed) If you have **buried** something, you have hidden or covered it up: It was so cold that she **buried** her head under the covers. *VERB*

delicious (di LISH uhss) When something is **delicious**, it tastes or smells very good: The cookies were **delicious**. *ADJECTIVE*

desert (DEZ ert) A **desert** is a place without water or trees but with a lot of sand. It is usually hot. *NOUN*

desert

drooled (DROOLD) To **drool** is to let saliva run from the mouth like a baby sometimes does. The dog **drooled** when it saw the bone. *VERB*

Ee

electricity (i lek TRISS uh tee) **Electricity** is a kind of energy that makes light and heat. **Electricity** also runs motors. **Electricity** makes light bulbs shine, radios and televisions play, and cars start. *NOUN*

481

embarrassed (em BAIR uhst) When you feel **embarrassed**, you feel that people are thinking of you badly because of something you said or did: When I realized that I had given the wrong answer, I was **embarrassed**. *ADJECTIVE*

envelope (EN vuh lohp) An **envelope** is a folded paper cover. An **envelope** is used to mail a letter or something else that is flat. *NOUN*

excitement (ek SYT muhnt) **Excitement** happens when you have very strong, happy feelings about something that you like. *NOUN*

experiment (ek SPAIR uh muhnt) An **experiment** is a test to find out something: We do **experiments** in science class. *NOUN*

experiment

Gg

gnaws (NAWS) When an animal **gnaws**, it is biting and wearing away by biting: The brown mouse **gnaws** the cheese. *VERB*

gravity (GRAV uh tee) **Gravity** is the natural force that causes objects to move toward the center of the Earth. **Gravity** causes objects to have weight. *NOUN*

greenhouse (GREEN howss) A **greenhouse** is a building with a glass or plastic roof and sides. A **greenhouse** is kept warm and full of light for growing plants. *NOUN*

greenhouse

Hh

halfway (HAF WAY) To be **halfway** is to be in the middle: He was **halfway** through running the race. *ADJECTIVE*

harsh (HARSH) To be **harsh** is to be rough, unpleasant, and unfriendly: The **harsh** weather made us stay indoors. *ADJECTIVE*

hooves (HUVZ or HOOVZ) **Hooves** are the hard part of the feet of some animals. Horses, cattle, sheep, moose, deer, and pigs have hooves. *NOUN*

Jj

justice (JUHS tis) **Justice** happens when things are right and fair. *NOUN*

Ll

laboratory (LAB ruh tor ee) A **laboratory** is a room where scientists work and do experiments and tests. *NOUN*

ladder

ladder (LAD er) A **ladder** is a set of steps between two long pieces of wood, metal, or rope. **Ladders** are used for climbing up and down. *NOUN*

lantern

lanterns (LAN ternz) **Lanterns** are portable lamps with coverings around them to protect them from wind and rain. *NOUN*

lazy (LAY zee) If a person is **lazy**, he or she does not want to work hard or to move fast: The **lazy** cat lay on the rug all day. *ADJECTIVE*

lodge (LOJ) A **lodge** is a den of an animal: The beavers built a **lodge**. *NOUN*

luckiest (LUHK ee est) The **luckiest** person is the one who has had the best fortune. *ADJECTIVE*

lumbered (LUHM berd) To **lumber** is to move along heavily and noisily: The old truck **lumbered** down the road. *VERB*

Mm

meadow (MED oh) A **meadow** is a piece of land where grass grows: There are sheep in the **meadow**. *NOUN*

meadow

mill (MIL) A **mill** is a building in which grain is ground into flour or meal. *NOUN*

monsters (MON sterz) **Monsters** are make-believe people or animals that are scary. In stories, some **monsters** are friendly, and others are not: Dragons are **monsters**. *NOUN*

musician (myoo ZISH uhn) A **musician** is a person who sings, plays, or writes music. *NOUN*

Nn

narrator (NAIR ayt or) A **narrator** is a person who tells a story or play. In a play, a **narrator** keeps the action moving. *NOUN*

Pp

persimmons (puhr SIM uhns) **Persimmons** are round, yellow and orange fruits about the size of plums. *NOUN*

persimmons

photograph (FOH tuh graf) A **photograph** is a picture you make with a camera. *NOUN*

Rr

relatives (REL uh tivs) Your **relatives** are the people who belong to the same family as you do: Your mother, sister, and cousin are all your **relatives**. *NOUN*

riverbank (RIV er bangk) A **riverbank** is the land on the side of a river or stream. *NOUN*

robbers (ROB ers) **Robbers** are people who rob or steal: The police chased the bank **robbers**. *NOUN*

robot (ROH bot or ROH BUHT) A **robot** is a machine that is run by a computer. **Robots** help people do work. **Robots** can look like people. *NOUN*

roller skate (ROH ler SKAYT) To **roller-skate** is to move by using **roller skates**, which are shoes that have wheels. *VERB/NOUN*

roller skates

Ss

shivered (SHIV erd) To **shiver** is to shake with cold, fear, or excitement: I **shivered** in the cold wind. *VERB*

shuttle (SHUHT uhl) A **shuttle** is a spacecraft with wings, which can orbit the earth, land like an airplane, and be used again. *NOUN*

487

slipped (SLIPT) When you **slip** you slide suddenly and unexpectedly: She **slipped** on the ice. *VERB*

smudged (SMUDJD) If something is **smudged**, it is marked with a dirty streak. *ADJECTIVE*

snuggled

snuggled (SNUHG uhld) To **snuggle** is to lie closely and comfortably together; cuddle: The kittens **snuggled** together in the basket. *VERB*

spirit (SPIR it) To have **spirit** is to have enthusiasm, courage, and loyalty: My sister has team **spirit**. *NOUN*

Tt

telescope (TEL uh skohp) A **telescope** is something you look through to make things far away seem nearer and larger: We looked at the moon through a **telescope**. *NOUN*

terrific (tuh RIF ik) To be **terrific** means to be very good, wonderful. She is a **terrific** tennis player. *ADJECTIVE*

Thanksgiving (thangks GIV ing) **Thanksgiving** is a holiday in November. *NOUN*

tortillas (tor TEE uhs) **Tortillas** are thin, flat, round breads usually made of cornmeal. *NOUN*

trash (TRASH) **Trash** is anything of no use or that is worn out. **Trash** is garbage or things to be thrown away. *NOUN*

trash

Ww

wad (WOD) A **wad** is a small, soft ball or chunk of something: She stepped in a **wad** of chewing gum. *NOUN*

weave (WEEV) To **weave** is to form threads into cloth. *VERB*

Tested Words

Unit 1
Iris and Walter

someone
somewhere
friend
country
beautiful
front

Exploring Space with an Astronaut

everywhere
live
work
woman
machines
move
world

Henry and Mudge and the Starry Night

couldn't
love
build
mother
bear
father
straight

A Walk in the Desert

water
eyes
early
animals
full
warm

The Strongest One

together
very
learn
often
though
gone
pieces

Unit 2

Tara and Tiree,
Fearless Friends

family
once
pull
listen
heard
break

Ronald Morgan
Goes to Bat

laugh
great
you're
either
certainly
second
worst

Turtle's Race
with Beaver

enough
toward
above
ago
word
whole

The Bremen Town Musicians

people
sign
shall
bought
probably
pleasant
scared

A Turkey for Thanksgiving

door
behind
brought
minute
promise
sorry
everybody

Unit 3
Pearl and Wagner

science
shoe
won
guess
village
pretty
watch

Dear Juno

picture
school
answer
wash
parents
company
faraway

Anansi Goes Fishing

today
whatever
caught
believe
been
finally
tomorrow

Rosa and Blanca

their
many
alone
buy
half
youngest
daughters

A Weed Is a Flower

only
question
clothes
money
hours
neighbor
taught

493

Acknowledgments

Text

Page 16: Text from *Iris And Walter*, copyright © 2000 by Elissa Haden Guest, reprinted by permission of Harcourt, Inc.

Pages 38–39: From *Poems for Small Friends* by Bobbi Katz, copyright © 1989 by Random House, Inc. Illustrations © 1989 by Gyo Fujikawa. Used by permission of Random House Children's Books, a division of Random House, Inc.

Page 46: *Exploring Space with an Astronaut* by Patricia J. Murphy, copyright © Enslow Publishers, Inc., Berkeley Heights, NJ. All rights reserved. Reprinted by permission.

Page 72: From *Henry and Mudge and the Starry Night*. Text copyright © 1998 by Cynthia Rylant. Illustrations copyright © 1998 by Suçie Stevenson. Reprinted with permission of Simon & Schuster for Young Readers, Simon & Schuster Children's Publishing Division. All rights reserved.

Page 100: From *A Walk in the Desert* by Caroline Arnold. Copyright © Alloy Entertainment and Al Jarcon. Reprinted by permission. All rights reserved.

Page 122: From www.factmonster.com from *The Columbia Electronic Encyclopedia, 6E*. Copyright © 2004 Columbia University Press. Licensed from Columbia University Press. All rights reserved. Reprinted by permission.

Page 132: "*The Strongest One* (Text)", from *Pushing Up The Sky* by Joseph Bruchac, copyright © 2000 by Joseph Bruchac, text. Used by permission of Dial Books for Young Readers, A Division of Penguin Young Readers Group, A Member of Penguin Group (USA) Inc., 345 Hudson Street, New York, NY 10014. All rights reserved.

Page 166: From *Tara and Tiree, Fearless Friends*. Text copyright © 2002 by Andrew Clements. Reprinted with permission of Simon & Schuster Books for Young Readers, Simon & Schuster Children's Publishing Division. All rights reserved.

Page 194: From *Ronald Morgan Goes to Bat* by Patricia Reilly Giff, copyright © 1988 by Patricia Reilly Giff. Used by permission of Viking Penguin, A Division of Penguin Young Readers Group, A Member of Penguin Group (USA) Inc., 345 Hudson Street, New York, NY 10014. All rights reserved.

Page 214: "Spaceball" from *Giant Children* by Brod Bagert. Copyright © 2002 by Brod Bagert, text. Copyright © 2002 by Tedd Arnold, pictures. Used by permission of Dial Books for Young Readers, A Division of Penguin Young Readers Group, A Member of Penguin Group (USA) Inc., 345 Hudson Street, New York, NY 10014. All rights reserved.

Page 222: *Turtle's Race with Beaver* by Joseph Bruchac & James Bruchac, illustrations by Jose Aruego & Ariane Dewey, Dial Books for Young Readers, 2003.

Page 246: From "The Secret Life of Ponds" by Elizabeth Schleichert, Illustrations by Frank Fretz. Reprinted from the June 2003 issue of *Ranger Rick*® magazine, with the permission of the publisher, the National Wildlife Federation®. Copyright © 2003 by the National Wildlife Federation®. Illustrations reprinted by permission of Frank Fretz © 2003.

Page 256: From *Easy-To-Read Folk and Fairy Tale Plays* by Carol Pugliano. Copyright © 1997 by Carol Pugliano. Reprinted by permission of Scholastic Inc.

Page 286: From *A Turkey for Thanksgiving* by Eve Bunting, illustrated by Diane de Groat. Text copyright © 1991 by Eve Bunting. Illustrations copyright © 1991 by Diane de Groat. Reprinted by permission of Clarion Books, a division of Houghton Mifflin Company. All rights reserved.

Page 306: *www.vispa.com*

Page 320: *Pearl and Wagner, Two Good Friends* by Kate McMullan, Illustrations by R. W. Alley, Dial Books for Young Readers, 2003.

Page 340: "Robots at Home" from *Robots* by Clive Gifford. Copyright © Kingfisher Publication Plc, 2003. Reproduced by permission of the publisher, all rights reserved.

Page 348: From *Dear Juno* by Soyung Pak, copyright © 1999 by Soyung Pak, text. Used by permission of Viking Penguin, A Division of Penguin Young Readers Group, A Member of Penguin Group (USA) Inc., 345 Hudson Street, New York, NY 10014. All rights reserved.

Page 368: From *Saying It Without Words: Signs and Symbols* by Arnulf K. & Louise A. Esterer, 1980. Reprinted by permission of Prentice Hall.

Page 376: From *Anansi Goes Fishing* by Eric A. Kimmel. Text copyright © 1992 by Eric A. Kimmel. Illustrations copyright © 1992 by Janet Stevens. All rights reserved. Reprinted by permission of Holiday House, Inc.

Page 398: "Do Spiders Stick to Their Own Webs" (text) from *Where Fish Go in Winter and Other Great Mysteries* by Amy Goldman Koss, copyright © 1987 by Amy Goldman Koss, text. Used by permission of Dial Books for Young Readers, A Division of Penguin Young Readers Group, A Member of Penguin Group (USA) Inc., 345 Hudson Street, New York, NY 10014. All rights reserved.

Page 406: From *Rosa and Blanca* by Joe Hayes, Illustrated by José Ortega, 1993. Reprinted by permission of Joe Hayes.

Page 420: From *The Crow and the Pitcher* retold by Eric Blair, Illustrated by Dianne Silverman. Copyright © 2004 by Picture Window Books. All rights reserved. Reprinted by permission.

Page 430: From *A Weed is a Flower*. Copyright © 1998 by Aliki Brandenberg. Reprinted with permission of Simon & Schuster Books for Young Readers, Simon & Schuster Children's Publishing Division. All rights reserved.

Page 454: "Products Made from Corn" from Ohio Corn Marketing Program Web site, www.ohiocorn.org. Reprinted by permission of Ohio Corn Marketing Program.

Illustrations

Cover Scott Gustafson

16–30 Christine Davenier

37–38, 158–159, 198, 213, 244–245, 275, 312–313, 339, 367, 397, 420–423, 453, 460–461 Laura Ovresat

68–85 Suçie Stevenson

128–150, 160 Courtesy David Diaz

152 Derek Grinnell

163–182 Scott Gustafson

Photographs

Every effort has been made to secure permission and provide appropriate credit for photographic material. The publisher deeply regrets any omission and pledges to correct errors called to its attention in subsequent editions.

Unless otherwise acknowledged, all photographs are the property of Scott Foresman, a division of Pearson Education.

Photo locators denoted as follows: Top (T), Center (C), Bottom (B), Left (L), Right (R), Background (Bkgd).

10 (Bkgd) © A. Witte/C. Mahaney/Getty Images, (C) Digital Vision

12 (Bkgd) © Doug Armand/Getty Images, (CR) © Phil Schermeister/Corbis

13 (TR, CL) © Ariel Skelley/Corbis

42 (Bkgd) © Shilo Sports/Getty Images, (BC) © Royalty-Free/Corbis

43 (TR) © George Hall/Corbis, (CL) © Museum of Flight/Corbis, (BR) © NASA

44 Corbis

45 (TR, CR) © NASA, (BR) © Royalty-Free/Corbis, (Bkgd) Getty Images

46 (Bkgd, T, C, B) Getty Images

47–51 © NASA

52 (B) © NASA/Roger Ressmeyer/Corbis

53–58 © NASA

60–61 Getty Images

62 (CC) Getty Images, (CR) © Royalty-Free/Corbis

63 (T) Corbis, (CR, C) © Richard T. Nowitz/Corbis, (BR) © Joseph Sohm/ChromoSohm Inc./Corbis

64 (T, B, TR) © Richard T. Nowitz/Corbis

65 (TR) © Franz-Marc Frei/Corbis, (BR) © Richard T. Nowitz/Corbis

66–67 © NASA

68 (Bkgd) © Jim Ballard/Getty Images, (CL) © Joe McDonald/Corbis, (BR) Digital Vision

69 (CL) © Nigel J. Dennis/Gallo Images/Corbis, (TR) © Michael & Patricia Fogden/Corbis

90 © Gabe Palmer/Corbis

92 (BL) Getty Images, (T, BR) © Roger Ressmeyer/Corbis

93 (T) © Roger Ressmeyer/Corbis, (BL) © Bill and Sally Fletcher

96 (Bkgd) © George H. H. Huey/Corbis, (CL) © Altrendo Nature/Getty Images, (BR) © Galen Rowell/Corbis

97 (TL) Digital Vision, (CR) Brand X Pictures, (BR) © Steve Maslowski/Visuals Unlimited

98 (BC) © David A. Northcott/Corbis, (TL) © Ralph Hopkins/Lonely Planet Images

99 (TR) © Tim Flach/Stone, (Bkgd) Getty Images, (BR) © David Muench/Corbis

100 Getty Images

101 © Maryellen Baker/Botanica

102 (BL) © Jeri Gleiter/Getty Images, (Bkgd) Getty Images, (BR) © Marco Simoni/Robert Harding Picture Library Ltd.

103 (CL) © Ron Thomas/Getty Images, (B) © Robert Van Der Hilst/Getty Images

104 © Paul McCormick/Getty Images

105 (BR) © Bates Littlehales/NGS Image Collection, (BL) © David Muench/Corbis, (CR) © Gary W. Carter/Corbis

106 (CR) © Charles C. Place/Getty Images, (TC) © Ralph Hopkins/Lonely Planet Images, (Bkgd) Getty Images

107 (C) © David Maitland/Getty Images, (TR) © David Aubrey/Getty Images, (C) © Jack Dykinga/Getty Images

108 (BC) Getty Images, (Bkgd) © Arthur S. Aubry/Getty Images, (C) © Steve Maslowski/Visuals Unlimited

109 (TR) © George D. Lepp/Corbis, (BR) © David A. Northcott/Corbis, (CL) © Joe McDonald/Corbis

110 (BL) © Farrell Grehan/Corbis, (Bkgd) Digital Vision, (BR) © Shai Ginott/Corbis

111 © Tom Bean/Corbis

112 © Joe McDonald/Corbis

113 (BR) Getty Images, (BL) © Jonathan Blair/NGS Image Collection, (CR) © David Muench/Corbis

114 (Bkgd, BL) Getty Images, (BR) © Michael & Patricia Fogden/Corbis

115 (TR) © Mel Yates/Getty Images, (BR, TL) Getty Images

116 (BL) © Tom Bean/Getty Images, (Bkgd) © Arthur Tilley/Getty Images, (BR) © Layne Kennedy/Corbis

117 © Matthias Clamer/Getty Images

118 (CL) © Tim Flach/Stone, (CR) © William J. Hebert/Getty Images, (Bkgd) © Ira Rubin/Getty Images

119 (BC) © Ira Rubin/Getty Images, (TL) © Royalty-Free/Corbis, (CR) © Jean Paul Ferrero/Ardea, (TR) © Rogier Gruys

120 © Steve Maslowski/Visuals Unlimited

121 © Ralph Hopkins/Lonely Planet Images

124 (CL) © Gary Braasch/Corbis, (BL) © Theo Allofs/Corbis

125 (CL) © Tom Brakefield/Corbis, (TL) © Bill Varie/Corbis

127 © Robert Van Der Hilst/Getty Images

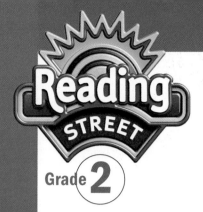

Indiana
Academic Standards

Standard 1

READING: Word Recognition, Fluency, and Vocabulary Development

Students understand the basic features of words. They see letter patterns and know how to translate them into spoken language by using phonics (an understanding of the different letters that make different sounds), syllables, and word parts (-s, -ed, -ing). They apply this knowledge to achieve fluent (smooth and clear) oral and silent reading.

Phonemic Awareness

2.1.1 Demonstrate an awareness of the sounds that are made by different letters by:
- distinguishing beginning, middle, and ending sounds in words.
- rhyming words.
- clearly pronouncing blends and vowel sounds.

Decoding and Word Recognition

2.1.2 Recognize and use knowledge of spelling patterns (such as *cut/cutting, slide/sliding*) when reading.

2.1.3 Decode (sound out) regular words with more than one syllable (*dinosaur, vacation*).

2.1.4 Recognize common abbreviations (*Jan., Fri.*).

2.1.5 Identify and correctly use regular plural words (*mountain/mountains*) and irregular plural words (*child/children, mouse/mice*).

2.1.6 Read aloud fluently and accurately with appropriate changes in voice and expression.

2.1.11 Know and use common word families (such as *-ale, -est, -ine, -ock, -ump*) when reading unfamiliar words.

Vocabulary and Concept Development

2.1.7 Understand and explain common synonyms (words with the same meaning) and antonyms (words with opposite meanings).

2.1.8 Use knowledge of individual words to predict the meaning of unknown compound words (*lunchtime, lunchroom, daydream, raindrop*).

2.1.9 Know the meaning of simple prefixes (word parts added at the beginning of words such as *un-*) and suffixes (word parts added at the end of words such as *-ful*).

2.1.10 Identify simple multiple-meaning words (*change, duck*).

READING: Comprehension and Analysis of Nonfiction and Informational Text

*Students read and understand grade-level-appropriate material. The selections in the **Indiana Reading List** (www.doe.state.in.us/standards/readinglist.html) illustrate the quality and complexity of the materials to be read by students. At Grade 2, in addition to regular classroom reading, students read a variety of nonfiction, such as books in many different subject areas, children's magazines and periodicals, dictionaries, and other reference or technical materials).*

Structural Features of Informational and Technical Materials

2.2.1   Use titles, tables of contents, and chapter headings to locate information in text.

2.2.11   Identify text that uses sequence or other logical order (alphabetical order or time).

Analysis of Grade-Level-Appropriate Nonfiction and Informational Text

2.2.2   State the purpose for reading.
Example: Read an informational text about pets to decide what kind of animal would make the best pet.

2.2.3   Use knowledge of the author's purpose(s) to comprehend informational text.
Example: Read an informational text that compares different people, animals, or plants, such as *What Do You Do with a Tail Like This?* by Robin Page and Steve Jenkins.

2.2.4   Ask and respond to questions (*when, who, where, why, what if, how*) to aid comprehension about important elements of informational texts.
Example: After reading a short account about the first man on the moon, ask and answer *why, what if*, and *how* questions to understand the lunar landing.

2.2.5   Restate facts and details or summarize the main idea in the text to clarify and organize ideas.
Example: Summarize information learned from a text, such as detail about ant colonies stated in *Ant Cities* by Arthur Dorros or reported about spider webs in *Spider Magic* by Dorothy Hinshaw Patent.

2.2.6   Recognize cause-and-effect relationships in a text.
Example: Read an informational book that explains some common scientific causes and effects, such as the growth of a plant from a seed or the effects of different weather patterns, such as too much snow or rain at one time causing flooding.

2.2.7   Interpret information from diagrams, charts, and graphs.
Example: Use a five-day weather chart or a weather chart on the Internet to determine the weather for the coming weekend.

2.2.8   Follow two-step written instructions.

2.2.9   Use context (the meaning of the surrounding text) to understand word and sentence meanings.

2.2.10   Draw conclusions or confirm predictions about what will happen next in a text by identifying key words (signal words that alert the reader to a sequence of events, such as *before, first, during, while, as, at the same time, after, then, next, at last, finally, now, when* or cause and effect, such as *because, since, therefore, so*).

READING: Comprehension and Analysis of Literary Text

*Students read and respond to a wide variety of significant works of children's literature. The selections in the **Indiana Reading List** (www.doe.state.in.us/standards/readinglist.html) illustrate the quality and complexity of the materials to be read by students. At Grade 2, students read a wide variety of fiction, such as classic and contemporary stories, poems, folktales, songs, plays, and other genres.*

Analysis of Grade-Level-Appropriate Literary Text

2.3.1   Compare plots, settings, and characters presented by different authors.
Example: Read and compare *Strega Nona*, an old Italian folktale retold by Tomie DePaola, with *Ox-Cart Man* by Donald Hall.

2.3.2   Create different endings to stories and identify the problem and the impact of the different ending.
Example: Read a story, such as *Fin M'Coul — The Giant of Knockmany Hill*, Tomie DePaola's retelling of an Irish folktale. Then, discuss different possible endings to the story, such as how the story would change if Fin's wife had not helped him or if Fin were not a giant.

2.3.3   Compare and contrast versions of same stories from different cultures.
Example: Compare fairy tales and folktales that have been retold by different cultures, such as *The Three Little Pigs* and the southwestern/Latino version *The Three Little Javelinas* by Susan Lowell, or *Cinderella* and the African version, *Mufaro's Beautiful Daughters* by John Steptoe.

2.3.4   Identify the use of rhythm, rhyme, and alliteration (using words with repeating consonant sounds) in poetry or fiction.
Example: Listen to or read the rhymes for each letter of the alphabet in *A My Name Is Alice* by Jane Bayer. Tell what effects the writer uses to make the poems fun to hear.

2.3.5   Confirm predictions about what will happen next in a story.

2.3.6   Recognize the difference between fantasy and reality.

2.3.7   Identify the meaning or lesson of a story.

Standard 4

WRITING: Processes and Features

Students write clear sentences and paragraphs that develop a central idea. Students progress through the stages of the writing process, including prewriting, drafting, revising, and editing multiple drafts.

Organization and Focus

2.4.1   Create a list of ideas for writing.

2.4.2   Organize related ideas together to maintain a consistent focus.

Research Process and Technology

2.4.3   Find ideas for writing stories and descriptions in pictures or books.

2.4.4   Understand the purposes of various reference materials (such as a dictionary, thesaurus, or atlas).

2.4.5   Use a computer to draft, revise, and publish writing.

Evaluation and Revision

2.4.6   Review, evaluate, and revise writing for meaning and clarity.

2.4.7   Proofread one's own writing, as well as that of others, using an editing checklist or list of rules.

2.4.8   Revise original drafts to improve sequence (the order of events) or to provide more descriptive detail.

Standard 5

WRITING: Applications (Different Types of Writing and Their Characteristics)

At Grade 2, students are introduced to letter writing. Students continue to write compositions that describe and explain familiar objects, events, and experiences. Students continue to write simple rhymes and poems. Student writing demonstrates a command of Standard English and the drafting, research, and organizational strategies outlined in Standard 4 — Writing Processes and Features. Writing demonstrates an awareness of the audience (intended reader) and purpose for writing.

In addition to producing the different writing forms introduced in earlier grades, Grade 2 students use the writing strategies outlined in Standard 4 — Writing Processes and Features to:

2.5.1   Write brief narratives based on experiences that:
  • move through a logical sequence of events (chronological order, order of importance).
  • describe the setting, characters, objects, and events in detail.
  Example: Write a story about an experience that took place during a certain season in the year: spring, summer, fall, or winter. Tell the story in the order that it happened and describe it in enough detail so that the reader can picture clearly the place, people, and events.

2.5.2   Write a brief description of a familiar object, person, place, or event that:
  • develops a main idea.
  • uses details to support the main idea.
  Example: Write a descriptive piece on a topic, such as *Houses Come in Different Shapes and Sizes*.

2.5.3   Write a friendly letter complete with the date, salutation (greeting, such as *Dear Mr. Smith*), body, closing, and signature.
  Example: Write a letter to the police department in your town asking if someone can come to your classroom to talk about bicycle safety.

2.5.4   Write rhymes and simple poems.

2.5.5   Use descriptive words when writing.

2.5.6   Write for different purposes and to a specific audience or person.
  Example: Write a description of your favorite book to recommend the book to a friend.

2.5.7   Write responses to literature that:
  • demonstrate an understanding of what is read.
  • support statements with evidence from the text.
  Example: Write a description of a favorite character in a book. Include examples from the book to show why this character is such a favorite.

Research Application

2.5.8   Write or deliver a research report that has been developed using a systematic research process (defines the topic, gathers information, determines credibility, reports findings) and that:
  • uses a variety of resources (books, technology, pictures, charts, tables of contents, diagrams) and documents sources (titles and authors).
  • organizes information by categorizing it into single categories (such as size or color) or includes information gained through observation.
  Example: After making observations and completing research at the library, write a report about animals that live in water or about different modes of transportation.

WRITING: English Language Conventions

Students write using Standard English conventions appropriate to this grade level.

Handwriting

2.6.1   Form letters correctly and space words and sentences properly so that writing can be read easily by another person.

Sentence Structure

2.6.2   Distinguish between complete (*When Tom hit the ball, he was proud.*) and incomplete sentences (*When Tom hit the ball*).

2.6.3   Use the correct word order in written sentences.

Grammar

2.6.4   Identify and correctly write various parts of speech, including nouns (words that name people, places, or things) and verbs (words that express action or help make a statement).
Example: Identify the noun and verb in a sentence, such as *Maria* (noun) *and a friend* (noun) *played* (verb) *for a long time.*

Punctuation

2.6.5   Use commas in the greeting (*Dear Sam,*) and closure of a letter (*Love,* or *Your friend,*) and with dates (*March 22, 2000*) and items in a series (*Tony, Steve, and Bill*).

2.6.6   Use quotation marks correctly to show that someone is speaking.

- Correct: "You may go home now," she said.
- Incorrect: "You may go home now she said."

Capitalization

2.6.7   Capitalize all proper nouns (names of specific people or things, such as *Mike, Indiana, Jeep*), words at the beginning of sentences and greetings, months and days of the week, and titles (*Dr., Mr., Mrs., Miss*) and initials in names.

Spelling

2.6.8   Spell correctly words like *was, were, says, said, who, what,* and *why,* which are used frequently but do not fit common spelling patterns.

2.6.9   Spell correctly words with short and long vowel sounds (*a, e, i, o, u*), *r*-controlled vowels (*ar, er, ir, or, ur*), and consonant-blend patterns (*bl, dr, st*).

- short vowels: <u>a</u>ctor, <u>e</u>ffort, <u>i</u>nk, ch<u>o</u>p, <u>u</u>nless
- long vowels: <u>a</u>ce, <u>e</u>qual, b<u>i</u>nd, h<u>o</u>e, <u>u</u>se
- *r*-controlled: p<u>ar</u>k, supp<u>er</u>, b<u>ir</u>d, c<u>or</u>n, f<u>ur</u>ther
- consonant blends: <u>bl</u>ue, <u>cr</u>ash, de<u>sk</u>, <u>sp</u>eak, coa<u>st</u>

LISTENING AND SPEAKING: Skills, Strategies, and Applications

Students listen critically and respond appropriately to oral communication. They speak in a manner that guides the listener to understand important ideas by using proper phrasing, pitch, and modulation (raising and lowering voice). Students deliver brief oral presentations about familiar experiences or interests that are organized around a point of view or thesis statement. Students use the same Standard English conventions for oral speech that they use in their writing.

Comprehension

2.7.1   Determine the purpose or purposes of listening (such as to obtain information, to solve problems, or to enjoy humor).

2.7.2   Ask for clarification and explanation of stories and ideas.

2.7.3   Paraphrase (restate in own words) information that has been shared orally by others.

2.7.4   Give and follow three- and four-step oral directions.

Organization and Delivery of Oral Communication

2.7.5   Organize presentations to maintain a clear focus.

2.7.6   Speak clearly and at an appropriate pace for the type of communication (such as an informal discussion or a report to class).

2.7.7   Tell experiences in a logical order (chronological order, order of importance, spatial order).

2.7.8   Retell stories, including characters, setting, and plot.

2.7.9	Report on a topic with supportive facts and details.
2.7.12	Use descriptive words when speaking about people, places, things, and events.

Speaking Applications

2.7.10	Recount experiences or present stories that: • move through a logical sequence of events (chronological order, order of importance, spatial order). • describe story elements, including characters, plot, and setting.
2.7.11	Report on a topic with facts and details, drawing from several sources of information.
2.7.13	Recite poems, rhymes, songs, and stories.
2.7.14	Provide descriptions with careful attention to sensory detail.

Looking Back: GRADE 1

Indiana

English/Language Arts

Academic Standards

Grade 1

Standard 1

READING: Word Recognition, Fluency, and Vocabulary Development

Students understand the basic features of words. They see letter patterns and know how to translate them into spoken language by using phonics (an understanding of the different letters that make different sounds), syllables, and word parts (-s, -ed, -ing). They apply this knowledge to achieve fluent (smooth and clear) oral and silent reading.

Concepts About Print

1.1.1	Match oral words to printed words.
1.1.2	Identify letters, words, and sentences.
1.1.3	Recognize that sentences start with capital letters and end with punctuation, such as periods, question marks, and exclamation points.

Phonemic Awareness

1.1.4	Distinguish beginning, middle, and ending sounds in single-syllable words (words with only one vowel sound). Example: Tell the sound that comes at the beginning of the word *sun*. Tell the sound that comes at the end of the word *cloud*. Tell the sound that comes in the middle of the word *boat*.

| **1.1.5** | Recognize different vowel sounds in orally stated single-syllable words.
Example: Say the sound that is in the middle of the word *bit*. Say the sound that is in the middle of the word *bite*. Tell whether this is the same sound or a different sound. |
| --- | --- |
| **1.1.6** | Recognize that vowels' sounds can be represented by different letters. |
| **1.1.7** | Create and state a series of rhyming words. |
| **1.1.8** | Add, delete, or change sounds to change words.
Example: Tell what letter you would have to change to make the word *cow* into the word *how*. Tell what letter you would have to change to make the word *pan* into *an*. |
| **1.1.9** | Blend two to four phonemes (sounds) into recognizable words.
Example: Tell what word is made by the sounds /b/ /a/ /t/. Tell what word is made by the sounds /fl/ /a/ /t/. |

Decoding and Word Recognition

1.1.10	Generate the sounds from all the letters and from a variety of letter patterns, including consonant blends and long- and short-vowel patterns (*a, e, i, o, u*), and blend those sounds into recognizable words.
1.1.19	Identify important signs and symbols, such as stop signs, school crossing signs, or restroom symbols, from the colors, shapes, logos, and letters on the signs or symbols.
1.1.11	Read common sight words (words that are often seen and heard).
1.1.12	Use phonic and context clues as self-correction strategies when reading.
1.1.13	Read words by using knowledge of vowel digraphs (two vowels that make one sound such as the *ea* in *eat*) and knowledge of how vowel sounds change when followed by the letter *r* (such as the *ea* in the word *ear*).
Example: Correctly read aloud the vowel sounds made in words, such as *ear*, *eat*, *near*, *their*, or *wear*.
1.1.14	Read common word patterns (*-ite*, *-ate*).
Example: Read words, such as *gate*, *late*, and *kite*.
1.1.15	Read aloud smoothly and easily in familiar text.

Vocabulary and Concept Development

1.1.16	Read and understand simple compound words (*birthday*, *anything*) and contractions (*isn't*, *aren't*, *can't*, *won't*).
1.1.17	Read and understand root words (*look*) and their inflectional forms (*looks*, *looked*, *looking*).
Example: Recognize that the *s* added to the end of *chair* makes it mean more than one chair. Recognize that adding *ed* to the end of *jump* makes it mean jumping that happened in the past.
1.1.18	Classify categories of words.
Example: Tell which of the following are fruits and which are vegetables: bananas, oranges, apples, carrots, and peas.

Standard
2

READING: Comprehension and Analysis of Nonfiction and Informational Text

Students read and understand grade-level-appropriate material. The selections in the **Indiana Reading List** *(www.doe.state.in.us/standards/readinglist.html) illustrate the quality and complexity of the materials to be read by students. At Grade 1, in addition to regular classroom reading, students begin to read a variety of nonfiction, such as alphabet books, picture books, books in different subject areas, children's magazines and periodicals, and beginners' dictionaries).*

Structural Features of Informational Materials

1.2.1	Identify the title, author, illustrator, and table of contents of a reading selection.

1.2.2   Identify text that uses sequence or other logical order.
Example: Explain how an informational text is different from a story. Tell what might be included in an informational book that uses sequence, such as a book on making a bird feeder like *The Bird Table* by Pauline Cartwright.

Analysis of Grade-Level-Appropriate Nonfiction and Informational Text

1.2.3   Respond to *who, what, when, where, why,* and *how* questions and recognize the main idea of what is read.
Example: After reading or listening to the science book *Gator or Croc* by Allan Fowler, students answer questions about the reptiles and discuss the main ideas.

1.2.4   Follow one-step written instructions.

1.2.5   Use context (the meaning of the surrounding text) to understand word and sentence meanings.

1.2.6   Draw conclusions or confirm predictions about what will happen next in a text by identifying key words (signal words that alert the reader to a sequence of events, such as *before, first, during, while, as, at the same time, after, then, next, at last, finally, now, when* or cause and effect, such as *because, since, therefore, so*).
Example: Read *Bats: Creatures of the Night* by Joyce Milton and discuss what words give clues about predicting where bats could be found or how they locate food.

1.2.7   Relate prior knowledge to what is read.
Example: Before reading *How Much Is a Million* by David Schwartz, discuss students' estimates of large quantities.

READING: Comprehension and Analysis of Literary Text

*Students read and respond to a wide variety of children's literature. The selections in the **Indiana Reading List** (www.doe.state.in.us/standards/readinglist.html) illustrate the quality and complexity of the materials to be read by students. At Grade 1, students begin to read a wide variety of fiction, such as classic and contemporary stories, poems, folktales, songs, plays, and other genres.*

Analysis of Grade-Level-Appropriate Literary Text

1.3.1   Identify and describe the plot, setting, and character(s) in a story. Retell a story's beginning, middle, and ending.
Example: Read a story, such as *Arthur's Prize Reader* by Lillian Hoban. Retell the story, including descriptions of the characters and plot of the story, by telling about what happens to Arthur in the contest that he enters and the one that he helps his sister to enter. Plot the story onto a story map.

1.3.2   Describe the roles of authors and illustrators.
Example: Read a book, such as *The Very Hungry Caterpillar* by Eric Carle or *Where the Wild Things Are* by Maurice Sendak, in which the art is especially important in telling the story. Describe the role of the author and illustrator, and discuss how the pictures help to tell the story.

1.3.3   Confirm predictions about what will happen next in a story.
Example: Read part of a story, such as *The Musicians of Bremen: A Tale from Germany* by Jane Yolen or *Lilly's Purple Plastic Purse* by Kevin Henkes, and tell what might happen next and how the story might end.

1.3.4   Distinguish fantasy from reality.

1.3.5   Understand what is read by responding to questions (*who, what, when, where, why, how*).

WRITING: Processes and Features

Students discuss ideas for group stories and other writing. Students write clear sentences and paragraphs that develop a central idea. Students progress through the stages of the writing process, including prewriting, drafting, revising, and editing multiple drafts.

Organization and Focus

1.4.1   Discuss ideas and select a focus for group stories or other writing.

1.4.2   Use various organizational strategies to plan writing.

Evaluation and Revision

1.4.3   Revise writing for others to read.

Research Process and Technology

1.4.4   Begin asking questions to guide topic selection and ask *how* and *why* questions about a topic of interest.

1.4.5   Identify a variety of sources of information (books, online sources, pictures, charts, tables of contents, diagrams) and document the sources (titles)

1.4.6   Organize and classify information by constructing categories on the basis of observation.

WRITING: Applications (Different Types of Writing and Their Characteristics)

At Grade 1, students begin to write compositions that describe and explain familiar objects, events, and experiences. Students use their understanding of the sounds of words to write simple rhymes. Student writing demonstrates a command of Standard English and the drafting, research, and organizational strategies outlined in Standard 4 — Writing Processes and Features. Writing demonstrates an awareness of the audience (intended reader) and purpose for writing.

Using the writing strategies of Grade 1 outlined in Standard 4 — Writing Processes and Features, students:

1.5.1   Write brief narratives (stories) describing an experience.
Example: Write a short story titled *My Friend* describing an experience that is real or imagined.

1.5.2   Write brief expository (informational) descriptions of a real object, person, place, or event, using sensory details.
Example: Write a description of a family member, a pet, or a favorite toy. Include enough details so that the reader can picture the person, animal, or object.

1.5.3   Write simple rhymes.

1.5.4   Use descriptive words when writing.
Example: Use varied words to describe events, people, and places, such as describing a day as a *sunny day* or *cloudy day.*

1.5.5   Write for different purposes and to a specific audience or person.
Example: Write a thank-you note to the store manager after a field trip to the local supermarket.

WRITING: English Language Conventions

Students write using Standard English conventions appropriate to this grade level.

Handwriting

1.6.1   Print legibly and space letters, words, and sentences appropriately.

Sentence Structure

1.6.2   Write in complete sentences.

Grammar

1.6.3   Identify and correctly use singular and plural nouns (*dog/dogs*).

1.6.4   Identify and correctly write contractions (*isn't, aren't, can't*).

1.6.5   Identify and correctly write possessive nouns (*cat's meow, girls' dresses*) and possessive pronouns (*my/mine, his/hers*).

Punctuation

1.6.6   Correctly use periods (*I am five.*), exclamation points (*Help!*), and question marks (*How old are you?*) at the end of sentences.

Capitalization

1.6.7   Capitalize the first word of a sentence, names of people, and the pronoun *I*.

Spelling

1.6.8   Spell correctly three- and four-letter words (*can, will*) and grade-level-appropriate sight words (*red, fish*).

Standard 7

LISTENING AND SPEAKING: Skills, Strategies, and Applications

Students listen critically and respond appropriately to oral communication. They speak in a manner that guides the listener to understand important ideas by using proper phrasing, pitch, and modulation (raising and lowering voice). Students deliver brief oral presentations about familiar experiences or interests that are organized around a coherent thesis statement (a statement of topic). Students use the same Standard English conventions for oral speech that they use in their writing.

Comprehension

1.7.1   Listen attentively.

1.7.2   Ask questions for clarification and understanding.

1.7.3   Give, restate, and follow simple two-step directions.

Organization and Delivery of Oral Communication

1.7.4   Stay on the topic when speaking.

1.7.5   Use descriptive words when speaking about people, places, things, and events.

Speaking Applications

1.7.6   Recite poems, rhymes, songs, and stories.

1.7.7   Retell stories using basic story grammar and relating the sequence of story events by answering *who, what, when, where, why*, and *how* questions.

1.7.8   Relate an important life event or personal experience in a simple sequence.

1.7.9   Provide descriptions with careful attention to sensory detail.

1.7.10   Use visual aids, such as pictures and objects, to present oral information.

Looking Ahead: GRADE 3

Indiana
Academic Standards

English/Language Arts

Grade **3**

READING: Word Recognition, Fluency, and Vocabulary Development

Students understand the basic features of words. They select letter patterns and know how to translate them into spoken language using phonics (an understanding of the different letters that make different sounds), syllables, word parts (un-, -ful), and context (the meaning of the text around a word). They apply this knowledge to achieve fluent (smooth and clear) oral and silent reading.

Decoding and Word Recognition

3.1.1   Know and use more difficult word families (*-ight*) when reading unfamiliar words.

3.1.2   Read words with several syllables.

3.1.3   Read aloud grade-level-appropriate literary and informational texts fluently and accurately and with appropriate timing, change in voice, and expression.

Vocabulary and Concept Development

3.1.4   Determine the meanings of words using knowledge of synonyms (words with the same meaning), antonyms (words with opposite meanings), homophones (words that sound the same but have different meanings and spellings), and homographs (words that are spelled the same but have different meanings).
Example: Understand that words, such as *fair* and *fare*, are said the same way but have different meanings. Know the difference between two meanings of the word *lead* when used in sentences, such as "The pencil has *lead* in it" and "I will *lead* the way."

3.1.5   Demonstrate knowledge of grade-level-appropriate words to speak specifically about different issues.

3.1.6   Use sentence and word context to find the meaning of unknown words.

3.1.7   Use a dictionary to learn the meaning and pronunciation of unknown words.

3.1.8   Use knowledge of prefixes (word parts added at the beginning of words such as *un-*, *pre-*) and suffixes (word parts added at the end of words such as *-er*, *-ful*, *-less*) to determine the meaning of words.

3.1.9   Identify more difficult multiple-meaning words (such as *puzzle* or *fire*).

READING: Comprehension and Analysis of Nonfiction and Informational Text

*Students read and understand grade-level-appropriate material. The selections in the **Indiana Reading List** (www.doe.state.in.us/standards/readinglist.html) illustrate the quality and complexity of the materials to be read by students. At Grade 3, in addition to regular classroom reading, students read a variety of nonfiction, such as biographies, books in many subject areas, children's magazines and periodicals, and reference and technical materials.*

Structural Features of Informational and Technical Materials

3.2.1   Use titles, tables of contents, chapter headings, a glossary, or an index to locate information in text.

3.2.9   Identify text that uses sequence or other logical order (alphabetical, time, categorical).

Analysis of Grade-Level-Appropriate Nonfiction and Informational Text

3.2.2   Ask questions and support answers by connecting prior knowledge with literal information from the text.
Example: When reading informational materials about science topics or social science subjects, compare what is read to background knowledge about the subject.

3.2.3   Show understanding by identifying answers in the text.
Example: After generating a question about information in a text, skim and scan the remaining text to find the answer to the question.

3.2.4   Recall major points in the text and make and revise predictions about what is read.
Example: Listen and view Steve Jenkins' book *Actual Size*; discuss his examples representing the physical dimensions of various animals and their habitats. Also discuss the artistic methods Jenkins used to represent the animals.

3.2.5   Distinguish the main idea and supporting details in expository (informational) text.
Example: Read an informational text, such as *Volcano: The Eruption and Healing of Mount St. Helen's* by Patricia Lauber, and make a chart listing the main ideas from the text and the details that support them.

3.2.6   Locate appropriate and significant information from the text, including problems and solutions.
Example: Identify the problem faced by a character in a book, such as *A Gift for Tia Rosa* by Karen T. Taha, and explain how the character solved his or her problem. Identify how problems can form the motivations for new discoveries or inventions by reading informational texts about famous inventors, scientists, or explorers, such as Thomas Edison or Jonas Salk.

3.2.7   Follow simple multiple-step written instructions.

3.2.8   Distinguish between cause and effect and between fact and opinion in informational text.

READING: Comprehension and Analysis of Literary Text

Students read and respond to a wide variety of significant works of children's literature. The selections in the **Indiana Reading List** *(www.doe.state.in.us/standards/readinglist.html) illustrate the quality and complexity of the materials to be read by students. At Grade 3, students read a wide variety of fiction, such as classic and contemporary literature, historical fiction, fantasy, science fiction, folklore, mythology, poetry, songs, plays, and other genres.*

Structural Features of Literature

3.3.1   Recognize different common genres (types) of literature, such as poetry, drama, fiction, and nonfiction.
Example: Look at the same topic, such as cranes, and see how it is shown differently in various forms of literature, such as the poem "On the Run" by Douglas Florian, the play The *Crane Wife* by Sumiko Yagawa, Anne Laurin's fictional book *Perfect Crane*, and the nonfiction counting book *Counting Cranes* by Mary Beth Owens.

Analysis of Grade-Level-Appropriate Literary Text

3.3.2   Comprehend basic plots of classic fairy tales, myths, folktales, legends, and fables from around the world.
Example: Read and discuss the plots of the folktales from around the world that explain why animals are the way they are, such as *Why Mosquitoes Buzz in People's Ears* retold by Verna Aardema or *How the Leopard Got Its Spots* by Justine and Ron Fontes. Plot each story onto a story map.

3.3.3   Determine what characters are like by what they say or do and by how the author or illustrator portrays them.
Example: Discuss and write about the comical aspects of the motorcycle-riding mouse, Ralph S. Mouse, the main character in Beverly Cleary's book by the same name.

3.3.4 Determine the theme or author's message in fiction and nonfiction text.
Example: Look at the admirable qualities in Abraham Lincoln as shown in both the fictional story *More Than Halfway There,* by Janet Halliday Ervin, and the nonfiction biography *Abe Lincoln's Hat,* by Martha Brenner.

3.3.5 Recognize that certain words and rhythmic patterns can be used in a selection to imitate sounds.
Example: Discuss the different words that are used to imitate sounds. To explore these words further, read a book on the topic, such as *Cock-a-doodle doo!: What Does It Sound Like to You?* by Marc Robinson, in which the author discusses the words that various languages use for such sounds as a dog's bark, a train's whistle, and water dripping.

3.3.6 Identify the speaker or narrator in a selection.
Example: Read a book, such as *Class Clown* by Johanna Hurwitz or *Dinner at Aunt Connie's House* by Faith Ringgold, and identify who is telling the story. Share examples from the story for how the reader can tell that it is told by that character.

3.3.7 Compare and contrast versions of the same stories from different cultures.

3.3.8 Identify the problem and solutions in a story.

WRITING: Processes and Features

Students find and discuss ideas for writing and keep a list of writing ideas. Students write clear sentences and paragraphs that develop a central idea. Students progress through the stages of the writing process, including prewriting, drafting, revising, and editing multiple drafts.

Organization and Focus

3.4.1 Find ideas for writing stories and descriptions in conversations with others; in books, magazines, or school textbooks; or on the Internet.

3.4.2 Discuss ideas for writing, use diagrams and charts to develop ideas, and make a list or notebook of ideas.

3.4.3 Create single paragraphs with topic sentences and simple supporting facts and details.

3.4.9 Organize related ideas together within a paragraph to maintain a consistent focus.

Research Process and Technology

3.4.4 Use various reference materials (such as a dictionary, thesaurus, atlas, encyclopedia, and online resources).

3.4.5 Use a computer to draft, revise, and publish writing.

Evaluation and Revision

3.4.6 Review, evaluate, and revise writing for meaning and clarity.

3.4.7 Proofread one's own writing, as well as that of others, using an editing checklist or list of rules.

3.4.8 Revise writing for others to read, improving the focus and progression of ideas.

WRITING: Applications (Different Types of Writing and Their Characteristics)

At Grade 3, students continue to write compositions that describe and explain familiar objects, events, and experiences. Students write both informal and formal letters. Student writing demonstrates a command of Standard English and the drafting, research, and organizational strategies outlined in Standard 4 — Writing Processes and Features. Writing demonstrates an awareness of the audience (intended reader) and purpose for writing.

In addition to producing the different writing forms introduced in earlier grades, Grade 3 students use the writing strategies outlined in Standard 4 — Writing Processes and Features to:

3.5.1 Write narratives that:
- provide a context within which an action takes place.
- include details to develop the plot.

Example: Write a story based on an article in a magazine, such as *Cricket* or *Stone Soup*, about what life was like 100 years ago.

3.5.2 Write descriptive pieces about people, places, things, or experiences that:
- develop a unified main idea.
- use details to support the main idea.

Example: Write a description for how to make a model boat. Include clear enough directions so that a classmate can make the model. Write a description of a favorite place using clear details so that the reader can picture the place and understand why it is a favorite place.

3.5.6 Write persuasive pieces that ask for an action or response.

Example: Write a persuasive letter to your family asking for your favorite foods on a special occasion, such as your birthday or a holiday.

3.5.3 Write personal, persuasive, and formal letters, thank-you notes, and invitations that:
- show awareness of the knowledge and interests of the audience.
- establish a purpose and context.
- include the date, proper salutation, body, closing, and signature.

Example: Write a letter to a pen pal in another country describing your family, school, and town and asking the pen pal questions about himself or herself. Write an invitation asking an adult to come to speak in the classroom. Write a persuasive letter to your family asking for your favorite foods on your birthday.

3.5.4 Use varied word choices to make writing interesting.

Example: Write stories using varied words, such as *cried*, *yelled*, or *whispered* instead of *said*.

3.5.5 Write for different purposes and to a specific audience or person.

Example: Write an article about the library at your school. Include a list of ways that students use the library.

3.5.7 Write responses to literature that:
- demonstrate an understanding of what is read.
- support statements with evidence from the text.

Example: Write a description of a favorite character in a book. Include examples from the book to show why this character is such a favorite.

Research Application

3.5.8 Write or deliver a research report that has been developed using a systematic research process (defines the topic, gathers information, determines credibility, reports findings) and that:
- uses a variety of sources (books, technology, pictures, charts, tables of contents, diagrams) and documents sources (titles and authors).
- organizes information by categorizing it into more than one category (such as living and nonliving, hot and cold) or includes information gained through observation.

Example: After making observations and completing research at the library, write a report that describes things found in nature and things that are found outside of nature.

WRITING: English Language Conventions

Students write using Standard English conventions appropriate to this grade level.

Handwriting

3.6.1   Write legibly in cursive, leaving space between letters in a word, words in a sentence, and words and the edges of the paper.

Sentence Structure

3.6.2   Write correctly complete sentences of statement, command, question, or exclamation, with final punctuation.

- Declarative: This tastes very good.

- Imperative: Please take your seats.

- Interrogative: Are we there yet?

- Exclamatory: It's a home run!

Grammar

3.6.3   Identify and use subjects and verbs that are in agreement (*we are* instead of *we is*).

3.6.4   Identify and use past (*he danced*), present (*he dances*), and future (*he will dance*) verb tenses properly in writing.

3.6.5   Identify and correctly use pronouns (*it, him, her*), adjectives (<u>*brown*</u> *eyes,* <u>*two*</u> <u>*younger*</u> *sisters*), compound nouns (*summertime, snowflakes*), and articles (*a, an, the*) in writing.

Punctuation

3.6.6   Use commas in dates (August 15, 2001), locations (Fort Wayne, Indiana), and addresses (431 Coral Way, Miami, FL), and for items in a series (football, basketball, soccer, and tennis).

Capitalization

3.6.7   Capitalize correctly geographical names, holidays, historical periods, and special events (*We always celebrate the Fourth of July by gathering at Mounds State Park in Anderson, Indiana.*)

Spelling

3.6.8   Spell correctly one-syllable words that have blends (*walk,* <u>*play,*</u> <u>*blend*</u>), contractions (*isn't, can't*), compounds, common spelling patterns (*qu-*; changing *win* to *winning*; changing the ending of a word from *-y* to *-ies* to make a plural, such as *cherry/ cherries*), and common homophones (words that sound the same but have different spellings, such as *hair/hare*).

3.6.9   Arrange words in alphabetical order.
Example: Given a list of words, such as *apple, grapefruit, cherry, banana, pineapple,* and *peach,* put them into correct alphabetical order: *apple, banana, cherry, grapefruit, peach,* and *pineapple.*

LISTENING AND SPEAKING: Skills, Strategies, and Applications

Students listen critically and respond appropriately to oral communication. They speak in a manner that guides the listener to understand important ideas by using proper phrasing, pitch, and modulation (raising and lowering voice). Students deliver brief oral presentations about familiar experiences or interests that are organized around a coherent thesis statement (a statement of topic). Students use the same Standard English conventions for oral speech that they use in their writing.

Comprehension

3.7.1 Retell, paraphrase, and explain what a speaker has said.

3.7.2 Connect and relate experiences and ideas to those of a speaker.

3.7.3 Answer questions completely and appropriately.

3.7.4 Identify the musical elements of literary language, such as rhymes, repeated sounds, and instances of onomatopoeia (naming something by using a sound associated with it, such as *hiss* or *buzz*).

3.7.15 Follow three- and four-step oral directions.

Organization and Delivery of Oral Communication

3.7.5 Organize ideas chronologically (in the order that they happened) or around major points of information.

3.7.6 Provide a beginning, a middle, and an end to oral presentations, including details that develop a central idea.

3.7.7 Use clear and specific vocabulary to communicate ideas and establish the tone.

3.7.8 Clarify and enhance oral presentations through the use of appropriate props, including objects, pictures, and charts.

3.7.9 Read prose and poetry aloud with fluency, rhythm, and timing, using appropriate changes in the tone of voice to emphasize important passages of the text being read.

Analysis and Evaluation of Oral and Media Communications

3.7.10 Compare ideas and points of view expressed in broadcast and print media or on the Internet.

3.7.11 Distinguish between the speaker's opinions and verifiable facts.

3.7.16 Evaluate different evidence (facts, statistics, quotes, testimonials) used to support claims.

Speaking Applications

3.7.12 Make brief narrative presentations that:

- provide a context for an event that is the subject of the presentation.
- provide insight into why the selected event should be of interest to the audience.
- include well-chosen details to develop characters, setting, and plot that has a beginning, middle, and end.

3.7.13 Plan and present dramatic interpretations of experiences, stories, poems, or plays.

3.7.14 Make descriptive presentations that use concrete sensory details to set forth and support unified impressions of people, places, things, or experiences.